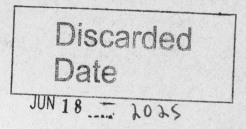

The Renovator's Primer

The Renovator's Primer

Meryl & Jeffrey Bennett

DRAKE PUBLISHERS INC. NEW YORK•LONDON

To our parents

Our thanks to:

Aboff's White Paint Stores
Eaton's Hardware
Larkfield Lumber and Supply Corp.
Jimmy Lynch
Ray Cole Aluminum Co.
United Ceramic Tile Corp.
Trio Designs, Inc. / Wallpaper Plus
All our friends for answering our endless questions
And especially Lenny, for the sweat and inspiration.

Published in 1978 by
Drake Publishers, Inc.
801 Second Ave.
New York, N.Y. 10017

Library of Congress Cataloging in Publication Data

Bennett, Meryl
    The renovator's primer.

    Includes index.
    1. Dwellings—Remodeling. I. Bennett, Jeffrey,
joint author. II. Title.
TH4816.B44   643'.7   77-87470
ISBN 0-8473-1663-7

Printed in the United States of America

Contents

Preface

In the most personal sense, our book is a reaction to the currently hysterical spread of a favorite old American cultural phenomenon: *Plastic City Incorporated* probably says it best. It encompasses the world of shopping malls, supermarkets, airports, motels, and freeways, and its boundaries are rapidly expanding. Like most citizens of the twentieth century, we recognize that technology and standardization are here to stay, and there is no longer the possibility of surviving without them. On the other hand, we find ourselves frustrated by the steady erosion of all that was personal and warming and lovingly irregular in the old way of life. We are realistic enough to concede that the clock cannot be set back sixty years, nor do we wish to see all the towns and cities in this country restyled to resemble small, nineteenth century New England coastal villages. What we do want to preserve is the *choice*, when we venture out, of going to an inexpensive home-style restaurant that is not part of a coast-to-coast chain; the possibility of shopping at someplace other than characterless, climate-regulated shopping centers; the option to live in a home that is not part of a network of identical development models.

Our discovery that these choices may still exist, that we might be able to preserve for ourselves some part of the world that we and so many of our friends care for without moving to a commune or subsisting on granola and lichee nuts was what motivated us to undertake the adventure that we describe in this book. We do not intend it as a work of philosophy, but we do mean to emphasize from the beginning that our purchase of a nearly one hundred-year-old Victorian home in Northport, Long Island, as well as the five years we have spent pruning, stroking, tending, petting, and affectionately restoring it, have had as their genesis a reaching back—a longing to return to the comforts and security and graceful beauty of an almost discarded mode of life.

As newlyweds, we were both determined apartment dwellers. Neither of us had ever even wielded a hammer. When we undertook buying a house, it was without much enthusiasm, and then only because friends had convinced us that after four years of marriage, a house was a more sensible investment for the future. But after a few Sundays of trudging through house after ordinary house, we wondered whether we weren't acting more out of obligation than conviction.

The turning point in our thinking occurred when we realized that "house" did not necessarily have to mean the sort of house we had grown up in. It did not have to overlook a parking lot (as did our apartment bedroom window) or a square postage stamp lawn across the street; it could overlook a bay dotted with sailboats and a thickly wooded peninsula. It did not have to resemble its neighbors on all sides; it could be a home of individual character. It could be spacious; it could be secluded, and, best of all in this world of dizzying inflation and recession, it could be affordable.

An older house suddenly became the right answer for us. It is becoming the solution for increasing numbers of people everywhere who share our desire to restore the charm of the past.

When we had made it through closing on the house we ultimately bought, four frightening prospects loomed threateningly, casting a shadow on all the happy advantages we had won:

• The house, although it had been checked over by an experienced builder and found to be struc-

7

turally sound, **was** *very* faded. Its moldings were badly damaged; the roof was buckled; the heating system was faltering; the floors were worn; the electrical system was inadequate; the grounds were scruffy; the basement was dank and foreboding.

• We could not positively distinguish a wrench from a pair of pliers.

• Our tastes were quite sophisticated.

• Our funds were severely limited.

The point here should be obvious. The tasks described in this book—the overall task, in fact— can be undertaken by anyone who is strongly motivated to pursue them. No inborn aptitude is required, no prior skills. Our experience is proof of that. Colossally ignorant we took up the challenge, and groped our way forward, learning as we went along. We were amateurs in every sense, but as many professionals we talked to along the way advised us, there is no more painstaking worker than a determined amateur.

The use of this book is certainly not limited to readers who want to renovate a century-old Victorian house. It should prove helpful to anyone who wants to remodel a particular room, who has any standard do-it-yourself task in mind, who wants a general introductory course in home renovation, who wants to save himself exorbitant professional contractors' fees, who has moved into a brand new house and wants to add personal touches that were not part of the builder's plan.

This is a primer in the most literal sense. Since it is the work of two people whose technical knowledge was and still remains minimal, we are addressing our text to rank beginners like ourselves. We assume almost nothing. To borrow an analogy from cooking, we would not, in our instructions on how to boil water, omit directions on how much water to place in the saucepan, what size flame to use, how to recognize when the boil has been reached and how to remove the pan from the stove. One of the greatest frustrations we faced in consulting published sources as we worked was the authors' assumption of the reader's familiarity with all kinds of exotic terminology, tools, and processes. We have made sure that if we err, it will be in the direction of oversimplicity.

The chapters are organized in two ways. In Part Two, where the actual renovation techniques are presented, the structure is basically uniform although variations are introduced wherever they seem necessary:

• An OVERVIEW, whereby the entire, often detailed, process is reduced to its essentials so the reader can focus simply on the exact sequence of steps he will perform;

• FIRST CONSIDERATIONS, a discussion of what must be taken into account before picking up a tool;

• SHOPPING SUGGESTIONS, aimed at helping to anticipate problems in dealing with retailers;

• MATERIALS, a complete list of all necessary equipment;

• STEPS, a clear enumeration of steps from the first through the last, including diagrams and illustrations.

In the other two parts, the form is more narrative, an anecdotal account of what our experience told us was valuable for others to pursue or to avoid.

By all means glance through an entire chapter before you buy any materials or pick up your first tool. Most of all, have a good time.

1978

Jeffrey Bennett
Meryl Bennett
Northport, New York

Part I

THE INITIAL STEPS

Chapter 1

House Hunting

FIRST CONSIDERATIONS

Once we had decided to start house hunting, we began quite slowly. We would examine the real estate section of the newspaper, following up only those ads placed by private individuals—which were not many. Since we knew nothing about buying a house, we thought it wise to stay clear of crafty real estate agents. Although we were later to change our thinking, at the beginning our strategy was sound. By going out on our own, we gradually learned how to interpret the real estate jargon in the ads. We also began to see what was available at different price ranges without the pressure of a salesman's presence and, in general, taught ourselves how to go about the difficult task of finding a house.

What Could We Afford?—The first problem we faced was deciding how much we could afford. We knew how much we had in the bank, how much we were now paying in rent on our apartment, and how much we earned in yearly income, but we couldn't translate these figures into mortgage payments. We did not know, for example, whether our financial situation meant that we could buy a house for $30,000, $40,000, $60,000, or whether we could afford to move out of our apartment at all. Eventually, through a real estate agent, we were helped out a bit. Through a mortgage payment table that agents and banks have, you can instantly discover what your monthly mortgage payment would be, given the cost of the house and current interest rates. A monthly figure is easier to analyze.

Location—The second problem was where to look. The only sound way of resolving this matter is to pose some hard questions and then decide where your priorities lie. Be prepared to sacrifice some needs to others:

1.) Is proximity to a large city a necessity? If so, then be prepared to pay several thousand dollars more than you would if the same house were located in a rural area.
2.) Does your shopping need to be within walking distance?
3.) Is the quality of the school system high? For families who have or plan to have children, this often becomes the number one determination.
4.) Must a railroad station or other form of public transportation be close by?
5.) Do you require a certain minimum plot of land?
6.) Can you be happy in a home located near or on a busy thoroughfare?
7.) Can you limit your search to one general area? We found that once we were able to confine our house hunting to two or three towns, the greatest hurdle had been surmounted.

A checklist can serve as a convenient guide, but you will probably not succeed with it unless you are willing to be flexible.

Old vs. New—We are making no secret of our preference for older homes. Indeed, the instant we decided that we wanted to buy and fix up an old house, a new spirit began to guide our every move. Most house hunters need no advice on the subject. Anyone who is strongly "new house oriented" knows his mind without giving it any second thoughts. Others appreciate the charm of an older home but are convinced the venture is not for them. We have several friends who admire the work we've done on our old home, who love old homes *per se*, but who insist that they have neither the patience nor the imagination to get involved.

The advantages of purchasing a new house are real. They do, because of their popularity, command a greater resale price; the basic support systems (electricity, plumbing, heating) will not need to be overhauled, and the walls and floors will not require patching or refinishing. But there are other features you can be almost certain never to find in a newer home. Consider the following items which we inherited in the ninety-year-old house we eventually purchased. They existed before we did one day's work on renovation:

• Three working fireplaces
• Large sliding wood doors separating the dining room from the living room
• A country kitchen with beamed ceilings, a built-in pine storage cabinet, solid brick wall with built-in fireplace, French doors leading to a patio, and pantry
• Exposed high staircase with a window seat on the landing
• Wide-beamed hardwood floors
• Screened-in front porch
• Rich, heavy moldings throughout the house
• A large, old-fashioned walk-up attic

Old can be beautiful.

CLASSIFIED ADS

Apart from a few inside tips from friends, virtually all your initial house leads will be drawn from the real estate ads in the classified section of the newspaper. Here are a few common sense points to follow in what seems like a deceptively easy task.

The organization of the real estate section of most newspapers is alphabetical by community:

MERRICK	Wooded Area
$27,990	BSMT, GARAGE
CARNIVAL OF HOMES	
868-6620	
MIDDLE ISLAND	$34,990
3 bdrms, heavily wded	
2 car gar, extras.	
MALLER REALTY	732-3311

NESCONSET—Nature's masterpiece on a half ac! Brick/cedar, sev rms, 2 bath ranch. w/wall, fireplace, gar, pool.
ANDREW F. DAVID   543-9400

Standard information includes: a description of the house and grounds, special advantages (don't expect to find a listing of the bad features), price asked (often negotiable), name and telephone number.

There may be more specialized information. Here are several ads for houses which the seller is offering directly to the buyer, without the services of a real estate broker. This means there is no middle man, no agent's fee to pay, and no outside pressure from a third party who is likely to profit as long as you buy something. It is common to see the words "owner" or "principals only" to indicate direct sales.

BAYSHORE: Two bdrms-baseboard heat, kitchen appliances, att garage. Enclosed with hedges and fence. $27,500   MO 5-1775

SMITHTOWN: Edgewood area. Damin Park colonial on green acre, 9 rooms low 80's.
Owner   979-6089

HEMPSTEAD W.—CATHEDRAL GAR.
Brk Col, C/H, 3 BR, 2½ bth, 2 car gar mid $50's.
Principals only   673-9119

Few such ads are found, and anyone who is determined to deal directly with an owner will soon find himself frustrated by the wealth of attractive offers that are controlled exclusively by agents. There are good reasons why as explained later in this chapter. Here are some typical agency advertisements:

AMITYVILLE   Five bedrooms, 2 baths, waterfront cape, 80 x 125, garage, 250 ft to bay,
$44,900
CORVAIR REALTY   226-3300

OCEANSIDE   Magnificent brick tudor, modern kitchen, 3 bathrooms, 2 car gar.
$59.900
AUBREY REALTY   766-6300

Once a prospective home buyer has established contact with a broker, he may either pursue a specific ad which prompted the call or, more likely, take advantage of any number of other leads the agent has on file.

The classified section is replete with abbreviations, some rather obvious:

BR's—bedrooms
bsmt—basement
col—colonial home
crptg—carpeting
fin bsmt—finished basement
form DR—formal dining room
LR—living room
mtge—mortgage
nr RR—near railroad
pvt—private
splt—split-level home
w/—with
w/w—with or without
wtrfnt—waterfront property

Others are more subtle:

A/C or CAC—air conditioning, or central air conditioning
attd gar—attached garage
cath LR—cathedral ceiling in living room
CH—center hall
cir dr—circular driveway
cor pt—corner plot
cust—custom made (or built)
E.I.K.—eat in kitchen
encl pch—enclosed porch
fam rm—family room
imm occ—immediate occupancy
ingd pl—inground pool
nr vlg—near village
oil H/W—oil, hot water heating
pnld—panelled
SD #26—children who reside in this house will attend school district twenty-six
splch—"splanch" (a design which combines features of the split level and the ranch)
s/s—storms and screens
suitable M/D—suitable for mother and daughter
WBFP—wood-burning fireplace
wded ac—wooded acre

You should also be familiar with a few key phrases which describe special circumstances under which a sale is offered:

takeover mortgage—Instead of securing his own mortgage from a bank, the new owner simply continues to make payments towards the former owner's already existing mortgage, with the remainder of the selling price paid outright in cash.

owner transferred—Present owner is moving, not because of dissatisfaction with the house but because his company has relocated him.

all applcs—Present owner offers all appliances in the house as part of the given price.

sacrifice—The seller is forced by circumstance to place the house up for sale and must sacrifice the higher price he feels the property is worth.

we have key—The real estate broker maintains that the house is rarely or not at all occupied and that the key can be obtained from him for inspection purposes.

exclusive with us—The real estate broker states that the house advertised has not been listed with any competing agent and is hence available through his office only. This may also be listed as *owner's broker*.

FHA mtge available—Present owners hold a Federal Housing Administration mortgage which they offer for transfer to the prospective buyer, or FHA terms available to new purchaser.

Finally, here are some typical things which might well make you wary:

• Generally, if the seller admits the house is a *handyman's special*, it's going to require *major* overhauling at considerable expense. Worth a look only for the very adventurous.

• In today's market, no house of a glowing description can afford to sell at a very low price. Call and look if you must, but there *will* be a catch.

• *Fantastic potential* is a suspect phrase. It clearly implies that the present shape is somewhat less than fantastic.

• An ad that has been repeated for several months straight means there has to be some reason for the lack of takers, despite the attractive price.

• If there's an eat-in kitchen listed but no dining room, don't count on there being one. Ditto fireplace.

The most unsettling experience of all is to locate an ad that lists every desirable feature you have ever hoped for in a house. The price is affordable, and the location is ideal. Then you discover that it had been sold eight days earlier and the ad not yet removed from the newspaper. It happened to us more than once.

WORKING WITH AGENTS

Real estate agents have, over the years, earned a collective reputation slightly to the left of used car salesmen. The comparison is not entirely inappropriate. Both professions deal in merchandise that is "big time" in the sense that people do not plunk down money for a car or home every day. More important, the amount of a single commission can be sizeable, so there is some reason for the desparation of their manner. And yet, there is an unfair side to this picture. As in any profession, there are likeable, qualified people and unlikeable, incompetent ones. Friends of ours, now in the process of house hunting, feel like one particular broker who has worked closely with them is part of the family.

Most real estate agents fall into three categories: those who work very hard for you; those who start out eagerly enough but who lose interest and patience if you don't buy quickly; and those who seem rather independent and even condescending.

Those who work very hard for you are the kind to link up with, but even with the hard worker there are things to beware of. First, be sure that they are not making work for themselves; they show you fifty houses because they have never caught on to what you really want. You may have to listen to them drone on and on about the virtues of a house you had dismissed from consideration at first sight. Our hard worker must have gotten so tired of showing us house after house that one evening he called us and said, "Get pencil and paper." He proceeded to give us a list of twenty addresses in the area we wanted, complete with a capsule description of each. He instructed us to get a road atlas and take a little drive for ourselves. If any house interested us, we could call him, and he would take us in. You may not be aware of how unusual that call was. Agents rarely do that, although we don't know if there is a written law against it. He was trusting our honest natures, assuming that we would not go into any house and try to make a deal on our own, cutting him out of a commission. For us, it was a blessing. It was much more peaceful to go around on our own, expressing our real feelings outright, and it saved hours of tramping through houses that we knew we wouldn't want to see. Ironically, we did not get our house through this salesperson. He did, however, direct us to the village and almost to the street on which we did buy our house.

The second salesperson is the one who listens to your requirements, makes pleasant conversation, and takes you out two or three times. On each occasion, you try politely to explain what is wrong with the house he shows you, but shortly you sense a gradual change in his manner. He becomes a bit less friendly, a bit more grumpy, and finally gets almost furious when you try, in vain, to explain that the house he is showing is across from a gasoline station, and you wanted one in a secluded, residential neighborhood. He does not call you again.

The third and least likeable type is the kind who sold us our home. He exerted no effort on our behalf, took us to only one house, and was so distant and patronizing that no one would ever have suspected he was really a local high school English teacher moonlighting as a real estate salesman. His agency did have a semi-exclusive listing for the house, and since we were buying a home and not looking for a friend, we nevertheless gave him our business.

We would rather have looked without real estate agents, but since that was the only way we would ever have found our house, we do not want to underestimate their value. As we hinted earlier, their major function is to show you houses that can only be seen and purchased through them. Most people wanting to sell their homes today don't want to be bothered with the tedious tasks involved—advertising in the newspapers, answering endless phone calls, and constantly staying home to show the house to prospective buyers. Agents can do all that as well as to direct customers to you who might not even answer a particular newspaper ad.

Most real estate offices carry two kinds of listings: multiple and exclusive. Multiple listings are held by any number of other offices. When a seller agrees to put his home on multiple listing, he does it through one agency, but a copy of the offer and a picture of the house is sent to all other agencies that are a part of what is known as the Multiple Listing Service. A seller who gives an agency an exclusive or semi-exclusive right to show the house may do so because he does not want an unlimited number of agents dragging people through his home.

If an agent is good and knows his business, he

can be more than just a salesman. He can give you information that, as a prospective homeowner, you should know. He can introduce you to new neighborhoods within your chosen area, and he can point out negative features of other locations that you might not learn on your own.

If your agent is really working for *you*, he can help you to negotiate with the seller of the house you choose, both as to price as well as for items to be included in the sale (e.g., appliances, carpeting, barbecues, and garden tools).

Note the following technique sometimes used by a *buyer* in dealing with various brokers. We have known of people who decided that they were not going to tell a broker how much they really wanted to spend for a house, reasoning that a broker will always try to tempt you with houses beyond your price range. So if they were really willing to spend $50,000, they would tell the broker that they wanted to see houses in the low $40's. Then when good houses came along, they would still be affordable. Although this technique may work sometimes, there are flaws in it. When we asked to see houses in the lower ranges, brokers took us at our word, and what we saw was awful. It wasn't until a broker showed us something for more than we thought we could afford that we found our house. There can be value in levelling with your broker.

GETTING FRUSTRATED

It is very easy to get discouraged in the process of house hunting. To some it happens because they go about it very casually, going out once every two weeks for a year, so that it seems as if they have been at it for a lifetime. With us it happened because we did our looking in a concentrated period of less than two months so that it seemed as if all we were doing was either looking at or talking about houses.

But the real discouragement comes with the houses themselves. Very soon you come to know just what to expect from the outside—you don't even have to go in. You will be able to recognize

the "cape" that has two small bedrooms upstairs with slanted roof and do-it-yourself walls; the old "grandma's house" with the all-too-outmoded kitchen and musty smell throughout; the attractive Dutch colonial across from a school bus depot. It is here that we share with you the advice of a wise agent: "A house is only as good as the neighborhood that surrounds it."

So, how many houses do you look at before you either buy one or give up? There is no answer to such a question; yet it is not an altogether foolish one. It expresses the utter frustration of the worn-out house hunter. Unless you are forced to settle by circumstances, such as a terminating apartment lease or the opening of school for the children, it is probably wise to re-evaluate your priorities and persevere. The right house may be the next one you see.

THE MOMENT OF DECISION

The moment when you look at each other and say, "This is it!" is not always a completely rational one. Sometimes, it is just a feeling you get about one house even though you may have seen others of comparable or better size, price, or layout. Eventually, the practical considerations must justify those feelings, however. Although it is possible to resell a house that doesn't live up to your expectations, it is not the same as returning a sweater. Just as good marriages are not always the result of love at first sight, so too, you may not fall for a house the second you approach it for the first time. Though it is not likely that you will choose a house that you hated at first, you may have had mixed feelings toward it. This was true in our case. The house looked "sort of interesting" as we pulled up with the agent, but the faded paint and buckling roof, along with the dull skies of a gloomy winter day, took away from some of the good features that were inside. By the time we left, the house was "really pretty nice," even on the outside, and in our excited call to our families an hour later, we elatedly told them about the "magnificent house" we had just found.

Chapter 2

The Purchase

FIRST CONSIDERATIONS

Once the crucial choice has been made, you naively assume that you have already bypassed the most challenging step in the entire process—finding your dream house. Although it is undeniable that your plans cannot proceed until you have settled on the house you want to buy, you're not really ready to relax or celebrate yet. Now you must prepare yourself for the world of lawyers, legal documents, and finance.

Unless dealing with bankers and lawyers is part of your daily routine, or unless this is not your first home, you are in for many surprises. Actually, if you are forewarned and prepared, you can approach the buying of a home with much less fear and discomfort than we did. You may still make mistakes, but at least you will not feel overly intimidated by such simple requests as, "Have your lawyer contact us in the morning."

Who knew that you had to have "your lawyer" in order to go house hunting? Of course, we knew that lawyers and legal matters were involved in the purchase of a home, but we never thought of securing one in advance. The attorney will officially come into the process within the first few days after you have located the house in order to draw up the contracts and then later to answer your questions and make closing arrangements. If you have already used a lawyer for other purposes, you might want to engage him again. Unless the lawyer specializes in a particular branch of law (corporation law, tax law, theatrical law) which causes him to have little or no contact with house contracts, he should be able to handle your legal needs.

If you are not related to or friendly with a lawyer, then you have at least two other avenues open to you. You can ask others for a recommendation or you can consult the telephone directory for the local chapter of the American Bar Association. They have a lawyer referral service that can help you.

TIMING MOVES

The right timing can make all the difference in life. There is no doubt that this is especially true when it comes to buying a home. Nothing can be more devastating than finding the ideal house only to discover that three hours earlier someone else had snapped it up. It can happen—it happened to us. One sunny winter afternoon, we had been following up a lead given to us by a real estate agent when we came to a beautiful old federal style house that really excited us. Our hearts sank when the agent contacted the owner only to find that someone else was in the process of buying it.

Nothing can be done to prevent someone from learning of an available house before you, but there are a few ways that you can place yourself at an advantage. First, when an agent calls you about a "hot property," go to see it immediately, if possible, and if you really like the house, lay claim to it by putting down a binder on the spot.

NEGOTIATING PRICE

Before anything can be put in writing, the price of the house must be set. This isn't always a straightforward matter. If you go shopping in a department store or order through the mail, each item has a price tag. House shopping, like antiquing, however, falls into another category—the prices are often negotiable. Like anything else, the specifics of your situation will determine the extent of your bargaining power.

No doubt you have heard the terms, "buyer's market" and "seller's market," and they mean exactly what they appear to mean. If you are lucky, you will be house hunting at a time when the buyer is at an advantage. On a local level, this may be when many houses are up for sale in a particular community. In a more general sense, a buyer's market also refers to a time when money is tight, and sellers are having difficulty finding customers.

A seller's market exists when houses are hard to find and when competition for them is great. Then you have little leverage in price negotiation.

The final and perhaps most important consideration in trying to strike a bargain is the actual worth of the house and property compared to the price tag. If the house is extraordinary, or if the price seems quite fair (occasionally that happens), then it may be unrealistic to bargain. If the house needs much in the way of repair, you might try to use that as a way to renegotiate the price.

Although almost everyone we know was successful in negotiating the price downward, we are embarrassed to admit that we paid full price for reasons involving both competition and a relatively fair price to start with. Above all, however, we threw logic to the wind because we loved that house and wanted it desperately. We have never been happier.

BINDERS

The term "binder," like so many of the expressions that we came to learn in our adventures with real estate ads and agents, was new to us at first. When you pick out a new car, you give the seller a deposit, but when you find a house, you put down a binder. Don't confuse this with the down payment which is a sizable sum amounting to something between ten and twenty-five percent of the cost of the house. It is the cash you must have in order to obtain a mortgage, and it is payable to the seller in two installments: about half when the contract is drawn up (called a deposit) and the rest when the closing papers are signed.

A binder is a token figure, usually between fifty and a few hundred dollars, which the prospective buyer gives the seller, either directly or through the real estate agent. A written receipt should be given, acknowledging the payment and listing the terms of the agreement. In most cases, the binder obligates the seller to hold the house at the given price for a specified period. You, the customer, are at an advantage here because the binder does not actually obligate you to buy the house. If you find a better house the next day, you can ask for and should get your binder back. Of course, your binder will probably be valid for only a short period of time, perhaps a week, unless the seller is willing to give you more time. To protect himself because his house theoretically will be off the market while you have a binder on it, the seller can take what is called a "second binder" from another customer (and a third, fourth, etc.) in case the deal with you falls through.

Don't be afraid to put a binder down if you say to each other, "This is it.". We lost our house at first because we wanted to come back the following day with someone who was knowledgeable about old houses before we put down a binder. Between 4:00 P.M. on Friday and 10:00 A.M. on Saturday, someone else beat us to it. We were devastated and hopelessly put down a second binder which, to our surprise, did get us the house a week later.

Occasionally, you may come across a seller who does not honor a binder or who gives you a hard time if you want it back. Be persistent in the latter case; remember, if you have his signature on a binder that makes certain promises to you, you can always take him to small claims court. Perhaps just mentioning it will cause him to back down. If the seller takes another offer, you can consult your lawyer if you are determined to have that house. The attorney will tell you what, if anything, you can do. See the appendix for a sample binder.

THE SELLERS

If it is difficult to make generalizations about real estate brokers or lawyers, it is impossible to generalize about sellers—*anyone* can be selling a home! However, you will always be dealing with people who want to unload what has so far been the biggest purchase of their lifetimes. Undoubtedly, they are out to make a profit—on you. The only way they can do that is if they have a really fine house to sell or if they can make it seem as if they do. Consequently, they may try to convince you that theirs is your dream house. Be polite but don't take their word for anything. If they advertise mooring rights, ask to see written proof; if they say the school system is excellent, do some investigation of your own; if they tell you that the roof is watertight, have an expert check it.

Your dealings with the sellers may also be influenced by time. Their frame of mind may be affected by the length of time the house has been on the market. They may be flexible with the price and the extras if the house has not sold immediately. If you see the house on the first day it is shown, and many other prospective buyers show interest, you may be at a tactical disadvantage. Time is also a factor when one party is in a hurry to close a deal. Either you or the sellers may be moving for business reasons, and the house must be disposed of by a certain date. Whichever party is in a hurry may have to make a compromise.

Another variable involves other real estate. Must you sell another house or condominium before you buy this one? Is the seller negotiating another deal with the money he makes from the sale of this property? We got our house because we were the only prospective customers living in an apartment, and the sellers, having already found a new home, were anxious to make a quick deal.

Finally, there is the not uncommon situation of a house being sold in the absence of the owner who may have moved or died. Whenever a house is unoccupied, you may be in a position to profit from the absence of someone who is personally committed to the house.

INSPECTION

House inspectors (whether they call themselves "consulting engineers" or "structural consultants") are in business to give you a detailed report on all the structural and functional qualities of whatever house you're thinking of buying. They usually operate with a checklist which includes: heating system, electrical system, pipes, walls, beams, woodwork, floors, roof, foundation, insulation, waste disposal, moisture and leakage, and exterior condition. The report, often as much as ten pages long, will point out the good features

of the house as well as the problems and, in the latter case, approximately how much it will cost to repair them. Then you must answer several questions:

Do the difficulties make the house a poor investment?
Are you interested in the house if it requires major repairs?
Can you still afford the house at the asking price?
Will the present owner be willing to renegotiate the price to account for the inspector's findings?

Of course, a formal inspection is not an absolute necessity. You can buy a house sight unseen if you like. If you are sensible, however, you will take some sort of precaution, even if it's just making a careful tour of the house with a knowledgeable friend or relative. This measure may be less foolproof, but it's certainly more affordable.

CONTRACT

Unless there are complications, when the binder expires the parties should be ready to advance to the next step, the drawing up of the contract. A meeting is set up between the buyer, the seller, and their attorneys (sometimes the real estate agent can be present too). The sellers' lawyer will present you with a standard form which has the particulars of the sale typed in. Names, address, description of the property, and price are all included as well as other usual provisions establishing the liabilities of both parties.

It is also usual for an additional page or pages called a "rider" to be attached, listing particular changes or addenda that have been mutually agreed upon.

Remember to put everything in writing. Whatever agreements you make, be sure that they are written into the contract whether they concern something as small as a garden hose or as big as a washing machine. Leave nothing to chance or the seeming good nature of the people you are doing business with.

Items to be sold to you or left in the house are not the only things that can be stipulated. If you want certain things to be removed, indicate those things too.

Until the day the previous owners move out, you will not know what condition the house will be left in. Some have it cleaned and made spotless for you; others, like ours, leave you with unimaginable filth. You can do something to protect yourself from such extremes, however. Make sure that you specify that the house be left "broom clean." This will not guarantee a floor "that you can eat off," but it will protect you from total disaster.

As assurance that the provisions of the contract are fulfilled, you can request that a certain sum of money (we settled on $500) be set aside at the time of closing to be released to the former owners only after they vacated the house, and you have checked it over. If anything is amiss, the money being held can pay for any replacements or repairs that must be done. Try to arrange for the money to be held by *your* lawyer. Then you won't have to go to court, as we did, to get the money, should repairs be necessary.

Once contracts have been signed, you are basically obligated to buy the house barring unforeseen circumstances, such as failutre to get a mortgage within a certain period, complications when the title is searched, or a problem with termites. The contract always allows you to have a termite inspection, usually at your expense; if termite damage is found, the sellers are required to make all necessary repairs, at their expense, or terminate the contract.

Besides signing the contracts, you must put down the deposit. The amounts may vary depending on the economy, the location of the sale, the cost of the house, and the kind of mortgage you hope to obtain. Today they usually vary from five percent for an F.H.A. or V.A. mortgage to ten percent for a conventional mortgage. At the time of closing, you will pay, in cash, the remainder of your down payment, making up the required ten to twenty-five percent that most banks demand before issuing a mortgage. The difference between the down payment and the selling price of the house, then, equals the mortgage you want to secure.

MORTGAGE

The two most common mortgages offered are the conventional bank mortgage and the F.H.A.

mortgage. A conventional mortgage is the kind you get from a bank or savings and loan association—probably what most people do when they have the money for the standard twenty to twenty-five percent down payment.

You might choose the F.H.A. type if you have a limited amount of money to put down—you need about ten percent of the cost of the house. You may, however, be charged a slightly higher interest rate, and your monthly payments will thus be somewhat higher. Also, to get an F.H.A. loan, the house must pass certain rather strict Federal Housing Administration construction standards.

Less common is the practice of taking over an already existing mortgage. Often a bank won't permit this because interest rates are likely to have gone up since the time the mortgage was first given, and the bank can make more money on a new mortgage. A bank that will let you profit in this way is rare indeed today. Even if the bank is willing, the new homeowner may not be able to afford this method in the short run. Specifically, he must be able to give the owner the difference between the remainder of the loan and the selling price of the house. Only if the previous mortgage is relatively new can such a deal be feasible for the average buyer. For example:

selling price:	$50,000
remainder of mortgage:	$27,000
cash you must have:	$23,000

The same buyer would need only $10,000 in cash if he got his own mortgage.

Finally, and only in desperation if all other avenues fail, you can turn to a mortgage broker. Such an agency has certain "ins" at banks and will help you, for a fee, to obtain a mortgage. The fee, naturally, varies from company to company, some charging a percentage of the mortgage figure and others setting a flat fee. If you choose this means, don't expect to get the lowest interest rates in town. An honest broker will even tell you that if you can get your own mortgage you should do so.

The ease or difficulty with which you obtain a mortgage will depend somewhat on your own circumstances and also on the state of the nation. In any case, dealing with lending institutions can be quite an experience.

Don't be surprised or overly offended if a bank

gets very personal with you concerning your money and your lifestyle. Even though they can foreclose and take away your house if you don't meet the payments, obviously they prefer to offer mortgages to low-risk people.

A big question asked by many couples today concerns the salary of a working woman—does the bank count it when evaluating financial qualifications. Thanks to either the women's movement or consciousness-raising, a woman's salary finally does count, sometimes. The exact nature of the woman's job is important here; if she has a profession, there is less of a problem today in many parts of the country. Children also play a role. A couple of childbearing age may have a hard time trying to count the woman's salary. At the very least, they may ask you if you plan to have children and, if so, how many.

The home you have selected is also of interest to the bank. Before offering you a mortgage, they have the right, at their expense, to inspect the house. Some banks are just not fond of old houses, but if yours is an oldie, don't get discouraged because not all banks feel that way.

Finally, the general economy of the country can affect the mortgage market. There have been times in recent years when it has been very difficult for people to obtain mortgages, and then the tight money situation will eventually ease up—no consolation to the people who had to search frantically to find a willing bank. Then the percentage rate at which the mortgage is given is likely to rise and fall, usually affected by what you hear referred to on the news as the "prime interest rate."

Although it is the bank that decides upon your qualifications, you can and should do some shopping around yourself. You do have some leverage in the mortgage game. For example, you can look for the bank with the lowest interest rate. It may not seem as if a quarter percent difference between banks matters, but when you consider that you are dealing with thousands of dollars over a very long period of time, even a quarter percent means a great deal.

You will also want to look for a bank that offers a fixed rate of interest for the term of the loan. Banks are not trying to push for a sliding scale which can only mean that your payments will rise, perhaps drastically, over the years.

The only thing that might keep you from applying to an unlimited number of banks is that most lending institutions charge an application fee. Each bank determines its own fee, usually at least thirty-five dollars and up. Some banks, to attract your business, will advertise, "No fee of any kind." All else being equal, this is an appealing offer which can save you a few hundred dollars in the end. Some of the banks that do have an application fee will credit you with that sum at closing and deduct it from their other fees if you do take the mortgage from them.

In the end it goes back to timing. Can you find the bank that will give the best deal at the moment you need it? Have you chosen a time when interest rates are going up? Did you just sign papers at one bank and then receive a better offer from another? In one of our few strokes of great good luck, we got in just under the wire at a time when rates were already up, and we saved ourselves a quarter percent per year.

CLOSING

The house officially becomes yours at a proceeding called the "closing." Whenever you mention the word to those who have already been through the experience, the first thing they will say is, "Bring your checkbook!" Yes, at this meeting, a great deal of money changes hands, and none of it goes in your direction.

The cast is the same as at the time of contract except for a few additions. At the closing, a lawyer representing the bank granting you a mortgage is there. Also present is a representative of the title company that has conducted the title search. A title search, conducted by an accredited title company, defines the boundaries of the property being sold and also certifies whether or not the property is capable of being sold: Do the sellers have any unmet obligations relating to the property, and are there any creditors who have attached a lien on this property because of these unmet obligations? If, at the closing, the title company reports that everything is in order, a deed will be issued to you upon payment of certain fees. These fees are for:

title insurance—a policy guaranteeing that the seller is the legal owner of the property and that there are no liens on it;
recording fees—to register the new documents with the county clerk;
mortgage tax—a state-imposed charge, found in some parts of the country, for the privilege of

borrowing money.

When the money begins to flow, not only do you endorse the bank check over to the seller for the majority of the money you owe him, you will have to pay the following:

to the seller—the balance of the down payment, the cost of the oil remaining in the tank if the house is oil heated, money for anything you are buying from him (appliances, etc.);

to the bank—a sum of money to start an escrow account which will cover the cost of the taxes on the house for a period of months, the fee for services rendered by the bank, if the bank requires them;

to the title company—mortgage tax, title insurance, and recording fees, if applicable in your state.

Just before we were ready to leave, our lawyer whispered to us that it was customary to give ten dollars to the man from the title company. We have not been able to find a rationale for this, but if you are forewarned, you can decide if you want to continue the tradition or not. We were so shocked, we just paid it!

If you contact your lawyer in the days before the closing, he should be able to approximate your closing costs for you so that they won't come as a total surprise. You might also ask whether he expects his fee at that time too—something you can't forget to include in your total expenses.

If, then, there are no slipups, after you have emptied your checking account and signed on all the right lines, you are the poor but happy owners of a home.

Chapter 3:

The Move

First Considerations

Alvin Toffler, in his bestselling book, *Future Shock*, reports that one out of every five Americans moves each year. If this startling statistic is true, we can all benefit by learning something about the moving process. One way to do it is the hard way, by previous mistakes, but transporting gear to a college out of town, setting up a bachelor apartment, or even establishing your first residence as a married couple can't fully prepare you for the more complicated task of moving into a house.

So when the contracts have been signed, sit down and read what follows: suggestions from two people who, collectively, have moved seven times including the "big one" up thirty steps from the street level to the front door of this house.

Breaking a Lease

Unless you are going directly from your parents' house into your own house or have been renting on a month-to-month basis, you will probably have to contend with breaking a lease. Few leases today contain a sublet clause which allows the tenant to re-rent the apartment. Thus, in theory, the landlord can hold you to the letter of the lease although he does have to try to rent the apartment if you give him official notice. In most cases, however, there will be a standard lease-breaking policy. Common procedures include:
forfeiting the security you gave when you first moved in; forfeiting your security and paying an additional fee (allegedly to compensate the landlord for the trouble of re-renting and preparing the apartment); a proviso that requires you show the apartment willingly to prospective tenants.

Often you will hear of someone who notified the landlord of his intended move along with his wish to use his security as his last month's rent, and does so regardless of the reply he receives. If you are fairly sure that the owner will benefit from re-renting the apartment, with a substantial rent hike, then you might take that chance. Necessity forced us to do something similar but not quite as daring. We wrote the landlord of our plan to move but never received an official reply. Not wanting to beg for a response but wanting to keep out of trouble, we paid the rent until we moved, left our security, and just departed. For a few months, the post office forwarded our rent notices which we ignored. Old neighbors told us that the apartment was taken about a month later, and we never heard from the landlord again.

Only rarely will you find a landlord who not only asks for no special payments but is willing to return your security intact—an unconditional release from all further obligations. We know a few people who were so blessed, but it happens very infrequently.

TO HIRE A MOVER OR NOT

Since almost everyone we know has bought a home within the last few years, we have heard stories of both do-it-yourself and professional moving, each kind having its successes and failures. If money is no object, hiring a moving company is a sensible idea. It may even be a necessity when the move is long distance. Otherwise, if you can gather a group of individuals not plagued by bad backs, and your pieces are manageable, you can rent your own truck when funds are really limited.

Although money was a concern for us, we had some very heavy furniture including a baby grand piano to worry about. Thus, we compromised: we hired movers for the large items and made several trips with a small rented van, taking anything we could easily carry ourselves.

Choosing a Mover

Consulting the Yellow Pages or a friend who has just moved are two good ways to start looking for a reliable company. Keep a pad handy as you make your calls, and in order to make a valid comparison at the end, you might ask each firm these questions:

• Do you charge by the hour, weight, or distance, and how can an estimate be gotten?
• Is there a charge for traveling time to and from the company headquarters?
• How many movers are included for the quoted price?
• To what extent are you responsible for damage done during the move, and how is restitution made?
• Is insurance available for special items?
• How much notice is needed to reserve a specific date?
• Do your people work on Saturday, if necessary?
• What if the weather is bad on the appointed day?
• How is payment arranged?

Whoever gives you the most accommodating answers will be the one to choose. We found, to our surprise, that the least expensive company was the only one listed in the Yellow Pages under both "Movers" and "Piano Movers" which was important to us. They included an extra man for the piano, offered special insurance for it, and did efficient yet careful work. Why the low price? The truck was a bit old, but other than that we can't figure it out.

If your move is interstate, you will probably want to employ one of the nationwide companies with a local agent. If the move is nearby, that is not as important. Local newspapers often have ads placed by private individuals who own a van and may be the cheapest of all. Be careful here,

however, especially when moving with delicate valuables. These people may be no more experienced than the friend from work who offers to help you in return for a few cold beers, and you may have to hire such movers at your own risk.

Long Distance Moves

Most of what has been said and what follows can be applied to long and short hauls alike. Of course, a long distance move is more complex. Timing, in particular, becomes a challenge. Your belongings are usually picked up on a specified day, but the delivery date cannot always be guaranteed. More than one household—sometimes up to four—is packed into one van, with the first one on becoming the last one off. On a long distance move, the moving company's dispatcher becomes God—the only link between you and your possessions. You would be wise to make your own detailed inventory, even though the company makes its own, to keep track of what gets put on *and* off the truck. It is not unheard of for items to go to the wrong family.

Because so many variables come into play here, it is hard to generalize. What you must do, as you screen the various nationwide companies, is to see which agency is most flexible. When you have made your choice, the agent will explain more fully the way that company conducts a long distance move.

The only other thing you should do on an interstate move is write to the Interstate Commerce Commission and ask for their booklet on moving. It will help you to know what you can and cannot transport from state to state, especially in the area of pets and plants.

PLANNING AND ORGANIZING THE MOVE

We can look back now with amusement and even a bit of awe at the notebook which we kept during the days between setting the moving date and the big day itself. We were so organized! "Yet to Pack or Move," "Calls to Make," "Packing Left for Saturday," "Monday's Calls," and "Special Boxes to Fit" were just a few of the headings. Yet they made a hectic time just a bit more manageable.

As soon as you know the move is definite you can begin to do the following preliminaries:

Start collecting sturdy cartons of varying sizes (none too bulky to carry easily) and begin to save newspapers. The best cartons, and ones that can be found with ease and in abundance, are liquor boxes and the corrugated egg crates with built-in hand grips. Otherwise you can buy cartons from some moving companies.

Pack up, as soon as possible, any items that are either stored away in the back of closets or are certain not to be needed.

Label all cartons specifically and try to pack similar items or things that belong in the same room together.

When packing fragile items, use lots of newspaper to line the bottom of the carton and to put around each piece and between pieces. It may be tedious, but you don't want to lose your valuables.

Discard, sell, or give to charity anything you don't want to take along to get it out of the way.

Notify all the necessary people or organizations of your impending move (it sometimes takes weeks for the change to go through). Don't forget to contact: insurance companies, schools, stores or companies whose credit cards you hold, utility companies, publications you subscribe to, banks, friends, and eventually the post office.

Make calls to arrange for the initiation or continuation of all necessary services in your new home. The post office or stationery store sells cards for such purposes, but another possibility for the business notices is to write a form letter, leaving blanks for specific names and account numbers, and photocopy it. You can then tailor its form to your needs.

Do the remaining packing, starting as soon as you think it feasible. Eventually, you will have closed all cartons except one which will have to be a catchall for last minute necessities.

Keep out some sheets to cover upholstered furniture, even if you are hiring movers.

Consider taking anything not going in the big van to your house in advance if it is yours before the day you are officially leaving your former residence. Obviously, this applies only to relatively local moves.

Check with the movers (professionals or friends) to confirm the moving date.

The Big Day

Let's be optimistic. Moving day dawns sunny and mild, and the movers show up on time! That is, in fact, what happened to us, and there's no reason why your move can't go smoothly too if you help things along a bit. Try the following, regardless of who does the moving:

As you wait for your movers, pack up any of the last minute items.

If you have children, make sure they are occupied so that you can supervise and/or participate in the move without distractions.

When the appointed time arrives, but the movers don't, be brave and call immediately, even if they are your friends.

If you are do-it yourselfers, add these to your list:

Once you have the truck and crew assembled, start loading the van. Follow a logical system so that people are not stepping all over each other and so that there will be enough room for everything without furniture sliding around or falling over.

Cover upholstered pieces with sheets *before* you take them outside.

If you have hired a moving company, keep these points in mind:

Before they start to load the truck, they will probably inventory the pieces being moved, noting any damage already there. Go around with them to see what is being recorded, even if you have your own list, and check theirs for accuracy before you sign anything.

Supervise the move without telling the movers their business. They know how to carry furniture and load trucks; what you can do is watch out for dirty hands approaching your white couch or point out items to handle gingerly.

If the company does not provide coverings for upholstered furniture, drape them with your own sheets before they are carried out.

Before the truck departs, make sure the driver has clear directions to your new address.

The Weather

Most moves take place regardless of bad weather, at least on short runs, because of advance scheduling. Rain will stop no one, even though there is a greater risk of damage to your furniture in wet weather, but in severe snow and ice storms, the companies and the drivers themselves may have different policies. Since weather forecasting is one of our least exact sciences, there is little you can do about the weather in planning your move. As we said, think sun!

Part II

GETTING TO WORK

In our description of just about every job, we arrive at a moment when four hands are suggested for the execution of a particular step: it might be the point at which one person holds the nut in place with a pliers while the other turns a screwdriver; when one person steadies a strip of wallpaper and the other brushes down the seams; when one person climbs a ladder and the other braces it. There's probably no place in the book where one worker can't manage the whole show. But when you operate as a team, as we have from the beginning, you immediately double your opportunities—both for sharing in the glory of the results and for partaking in some truly spectacular fights. And fights there will most surely be, unless either of you is blessed with the disposition of a lamb.

There are three golden rules of etiquette which apply here, but even more than with the other common social graces, you will find that they exist only to be broken:

Always make polite requests for the exchange of equipment. Early in the game, we used to say "Excuse me, but do you think you could hand me the hammer?" These days, it's become "Hammer!" Both of us now understand, accept, and welcome the shorthand.

Always be patient in the demands you make of your work partner. Egos can conflict dangerously on team projects.

Always be realistic in your demands for perfection. On our first full afternoon of work, we spent a good four hours power sanding the wood trim in our 7' x 3' pantry. Every last nick and scratch had to be smoothed into oblivion. Those who value their mental health soon learn to bend these absolute demands.

Chapter 4

The Basics

Of the whole range of equipment available to the home renovator, a lot less than you'd imagine, as few as twenty tools, are necessary. The day may come when you feel ready to graduate to more advanced projects, and that's the time for buying a bandsaw, a lathe, or a drill press. Our collection fits (albeit snugly) into a 7″ x 14″ x 4″ carpenter's box, with a power drill, sander, jigsaw, vise, and a few handsaws being the only added extras.

In buying and maintaining the tools, remember two points, both of them well-worn cliches: buy good quality tools, and keep them in decent shape. You need not spend a fortune on tools, but you should be thinking of the long-range quality of the hammer you buy, not just its immediate function. A cheap model whose handle comes loose from the head after three years is not the one you want. As a philosopher friend often reminds us, "Cheap is dear in the end."

For organizing all your gear, it is much easier to offer advice than to follow it. In our house, the hand tools are tricky to locate since they are crammed, in no particular order, into one all-purpose box that has no permanent home. Closed paint cans are piled on the ledge next to the cellar stairs, and equipment of all kind is stored in whatever room still sits waiting to be renovated. This is an imperfect arrangement, and we are not proud of our careless ways. Naturally, it is a far better idea to organize everything you own in one convenient area, usually the basement, on neatly arranged shelves and in drawers.

Keeping your equipment in good condition involves less effort, but here there's no escaping the necessity. Set aside one old hammer and one old screwdriver, and heap on them all the abuses your spirit dictates: prying open paint cans or freeing a bureau drawer that's stuck. But protect the others by using them to do only the jobs they were designed to do. Moisture is the enemy of good tools. The rust will build up more easily than it will come loose. So choose a dry space (In our basement, we keep two dehumidifiers going for more than half of the year.), coat your tools, especially the saws, lightly with oil from time to time, and keep them clean.

The annotated lists that follow are basic. If you own these materials, you should be able to complete any home renovation chore described in this book, as well as many more. Don't think that you have to gather it all in one stupendous shopping spree. The sanest way is to get what you need for whatever job you're doing, and then add periodically as you go along.

We have consciously omitted from these lists such items as large drum sanders and heavy duty power saws which you can rent if necessary. As you read, if you come to the name of a tool that is unfamiliar, look back or ahead, and you'll find it described separately. Certain specialized tools, though, such as a notched trowel or a seam roller for smoothing wallpaper, are used only for very specific jobs, and you will find them discussed in later chapters.

THE ESSENTIAL TOOLS

Hammer

There are many kinds of hammers, but you need only a simple claw type with forged steel head and hickory handle. This most basic of all tools often gets used for any number of questionable jobs—prying open old glue cans, loosening stuck windows—but, in fact, it is designed for two purposes only: driving a nail into a surface or drawing it out.

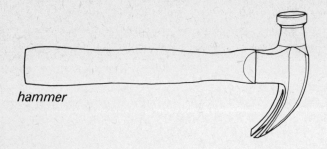
hammer

Screwdriver

One standard and one Phillips screwdriver (for screw heads with a slotted cross) are sufficient for almost any basic job. We've collected six, though, with shanks ranging from 1½" to 6" and blade widths from ⅛" to 5/16" because we have had to drive and remove a great variety of screws.

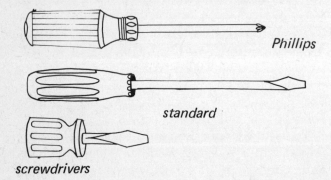
Phillips

standard

screwdrivers

Saw

You should own three kinds of saws: a ripsaw for cutting along the length of a piece of wood (*with* the grain), a crosscut saw for cutting across the width (*against* the grain), and a hacksaw, with adjustable and replaceable blades, for light sawing through metals, such as chain links, screws, or heavy wire. A backsaw is usually used in combination with a miter box to make angled cuts in wood trim.

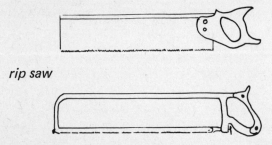
rip saw

hacksaw

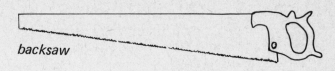
backsaw

Drill

You use a drill to bore holes in wood, metal, or any other suitable material. The classic tool is the carpenter's brace and bit, pictured below, but the electric drill, being infinitely more efficient and practical, has become a virtual necessity nowadays. You'll probably find yourself working with it much more frequently than the brace and bit which, ironically, is a handier tool for removing stubborn screws than for drilling.

The standard all-purpose electric drill should be double insulated (to prevent shock) with a ⅜" capacity. All that means is that the chuck—the adjustable jaws which grip the drill bit—can accept bits with a shank up to ⅜" thick. The tool is activated by squeezing a trigger, and it's probably a good idea to buy a reversible one with a variable speed adjustment, since the bit should rotate faster or slower depending on the hardness of the material you're drilling into.

The reversible feature is necessary if you eventually decide to buy a set of screwdriver attachments for your drill. For starters, though, a graduated set of high speed steel twist bits, which are usable with both wood *and* metal, is all you'll need. They usually range in size from 1/16" to ½".

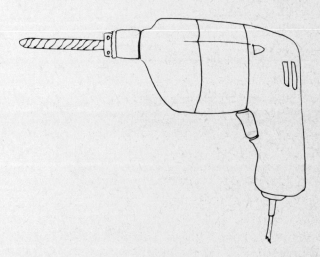
drill

Pliers

Pliers are tools designed to grip various materials in situations where your fingers aren't strong enough. Many varieties can also do cutting, the combination slip-joint pliers, for example. Our tool box contains two kinds.

The *combination slip-joint pliers* combines the best features of the standard slip-joint pliers (sometimes called double-joint or mechanics pliers) and the side cutting pliers (sometimes called wire cutters). Don't let the nomenclature discourage you. Just think of the combination pliers as one tool that performs the function of two. When you want to grab large objects, open the jaws to the fullest extent and they will lock back into the spread position. To grip smaller objects, again open the jaws to the fullest extent, and they will return to the closed position. These pliers can help you to keep a nut steady when you're removing a bolt or to screw in a small hook when the thumb and index finger fail. An added benefit is that the inside surface of each jaw is a cutting edge, so that if you place a length of wire way back into the opening, the pliers will work just like side cutters. To cut a wire, simply hold it in one hand and the pliers in the other, and squeeze the handles together until you break through. To strip a wire, which means to remove the plastic insulation from the tip so as to expose the copper inside, set the wire way back in the jaws, but this time squeeze gently, just enough to break through the insulation, not the metal. You can then give the wire a half turn to sever any remaining plastic from the other side of the wire, and pull it off with your hands.

The *long nose pliers* (many of the home repair books say "needle nose") are for getting into tight spaces that you otherwise couldn't reach. They are indispensable, not just to invade remote corners, but for all sorts of miscellaneous tasks, like holding a small nut steady while inserting a bolt.

You can cause permanent damage by over-taxing a pair of pliers or by using them for the wrong job. For example, pliers are not the thing to use for removing a nut from a bolt. That's the job of the wrench which is a stronger tool. Apply too much of the wrong kind of pressure and you will "spring" the jaws, and thereafter the pliers will be fit for nothing more than a shelf decoration.

Wrench

Wrenches are twisting tools, and, basically, you'll be using them to loosen or tighten nuts or bolt heads. They are used most often in plumbing, which probably explains why we haven't touched ours in years. The one you buy should be an adjustable crescent wrench, somewhere between 8" and 10" long, with jaws that open to a 2" capacity. It should also be labelled *drop forged*, which means that the steel was compressed with a heavy weight for extra strength and hardness while it was still molten.

To use the wrench correctly, make sure that the jaws are adjusted firmly against the nut so that the tool won't slip. In general, turn clockwise to tighten, counter-clockwise to loosen, but check to be sure you're grunting and sweating in the right direction. One more tip: position the wrench so that in turning, you are always exerting pressure against the lower, adjustable jaw, not the upper stationary one.

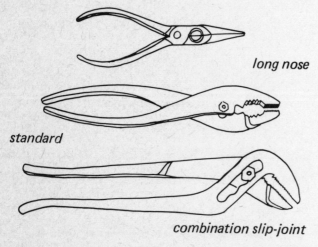

long nose

standard

combination slip-joint

pliers

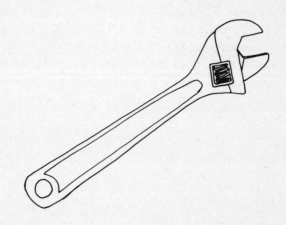

wrench

There are sometimes awkward situations when, in order to use one wrench to loosen a nut, you need another wrench to hold the bolt (or whatever else) steady. At such times, you'll need two wrenches and four hands for the job.

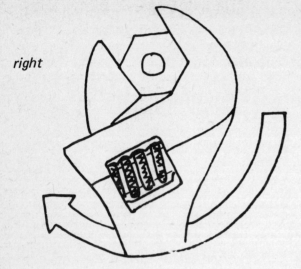

right

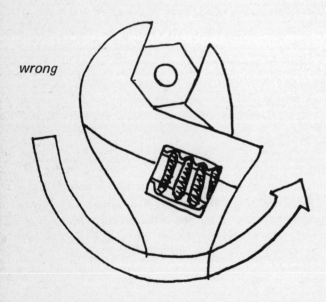

wrong

Tape Measure

Buy a 12' steel tape measure with a spring return, one that can lock in place anywhere you choose so you don't have to tie up one hand to hold the end steady. In general, the tape should be rigid enough to keep its shape, but thin enough so that the markings lie as close as possible to the working surface.

tape measure

Square

It is an act of foolish bravado to think you can just as easily mark off a right angle with your eye as with a carpenter's square (also called a framing square). We've tried and paid the price. Also, never presume that the corners of your ceilings and floors are true perpendiculars. Squares were around when most old houses were built but apparently were not always used. Double check to make sure.

There are all sorts of fancy combination squares available, as well as the familiar try square, but the 16'' x 24'' steel framing square pictured here is your best bet because you can use it against almost any flat surface, and the angle has a relatively long extension.

Yard Stick

This is not an ultra-precision instrument, but when you need a solid measuring tool—to draw a line across a piece of wallpaper, for example—this is your choice. Paint stores sometimes give flimsy, cheap ones away free, but it's probably worthwhile to invest in something sturdy.

yardstick

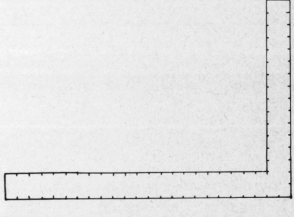

square

Level

Use this tool to see whether a line or surface is truly horizontal or vertical (instead of just looking horizontal or vertical). The level consists of a frame into which are built one, two, or more glass tubes filled with liquid containing a bubble. The bubble floats around as you move the frame, but when the level lies perfectly flat or plumb, it will sit *exactly* inside the two black lines on the tube. We recommend that you invest in the two-foot, three-bubble aluminum model that will enable you to check for horizontal and vertical at the same time.

level

Awl

It takes a few years of practical experience to learn the differences between the awl, the nailset, and the ice pick. The awl is an indispensable tool used whenever you want to bore a starter hole for a woodscrew. In fact, don't try sinking a screw without using one. Place it at right angles to the board, and strike it with a hammer once or twice before you use your drill. This will prevent the bit from wandering off course.

If you don't own a power drill, you'll find a threaded awl excellent for small screws. It's the same tool, but this time the shaft is threaded so the awl can bore the entire starter hole for you. Twist it into the surface of the wood to a depth just below the full length of the screw; remove it, and then insert the screw.

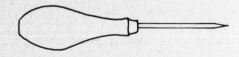

awl

Nailset

Use this simple tool to do exactly what its name implies: set a nail, a finishing nail, to be specific. The finishing nail is the one with the small head designed to be struck by the nailset below the surface of a board. Notice that the finishing nail has a slight indentation on its head into which the nailset can sit comfortably. Hold it at right angles to the wood, straight on top of the nail, and tap the head once or twice with your hammer so the head no longer shows. If you are a perfectionist, you can plug the hole with plastic wood to conceal the nail completely.

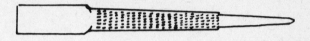

nailset

Ice Pick

Once used for picking ice, this tool is handy for a multitude of odd jobs: boring starter holes, testing wood timbers for termite damage, punching tiny holes in the rim of a paint can so the paint doesn't clump up around the rim.

ice pick

Staple Gun

You probably won't find a staple gun listed as a tool in any of the classic handyman's books, but we've found it invaluable when it comes to securing a wire, installing insulation, and replacing a screen. Buy the large, heavy duty kind. The so-called "tack guns" are too delicate for most jobs.

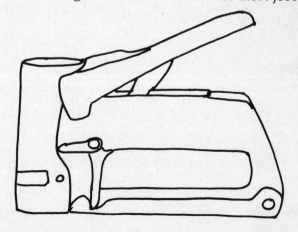

staple gun

Utility Knife: Matte Knife, Scoring Knife, Shop Knife

Good for scoring sheetrock if you don't have a jigsaw, a utility knife is also used for trimming wallpaper. By loosening the center screw you can open the knife and replace the adjustable blade when it gets dull. For safety's sake, buy one that has a retractable blade.

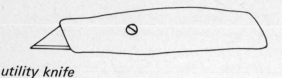

utility knife

Utility Scissors

A good strong pair of scissors is worth having, just for cutting up rags, sandpaper, or wire. You can also use them on vinyl tiles, that have been softened by heating, for cutting irregular shapes.

utility scissors

Scraping Knives

As is so often the case, two and three names are often used interchangeably to refer to the same tool. Do you call it a spackling knife, a putty knife, a taping knife, or a scraper? There are differences, in fact, but they are largely a matter of the width and strength of the blade. Next to our hammer and screwdriver, we've used these more than any other tools in our kit. Buy ones with stiff blades.

1¼" Putty Knife—Should have some flexibility. Used for patching plaster and sheetrock, replacing glass window panes, prying loose damaged floorboards, and scores of other jobs you're certain to invent for it.

3" Putty Knife (Spackling Knife)—Used for covering seams in sheetrock walls, spackling in dents and chips of some size, and scraping off old paint.

Large Scraper—Used for scraping off old paint or wallpaper, smoothing wallpaper into corners, etc.

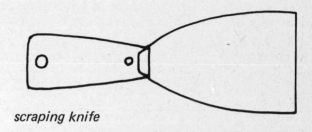

scraping knife

Power Finishing Sander: Orbital Sander, Oscillating Sander

This is the second power tool you should buy. Of the different types of sanders, you have only one practical choice here. The belt sanders are too unwieldy for general use and give too rough a cut. They're designed for heavy work like floor refinishing. If you need one, it's best to rent it. The disc sanders work in a circular motion. While they're okay for preparing a wall for painting or edging a wood floor, they, too, are unsuitable for fine work. What you *do* want is called a power finishing sander, although with typical confusion, you will also hear it referred to as an orbital sander, oscillating sander, or vibrating sander.

It operates with continuous back and forth motion (Actually, the pad is vibrating in a tiny, imperceptible orbit.) which allows for maximum smoothness, even if you can't do the same kind of heavy work as with the others.

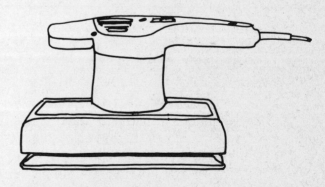

power finishing sander

Saber Saw, Portable Jigsaw

A worthwhile investment for light cutting of wood and metal, a saber saw is a good tool to own because of its enormous versatility; once you feel secure with it, you can use it for cross-cutting, rip-cutting, fancy cuts and curves, especially on plywood, and sheetrock. Being reasonably lazy, we find ourselves picking it up at times when we'd probably be better off with a handsaw.

You don't want to try the saber saw, however, on a piece of 6" x 6" timber. That's the province of the circular saw, a heavy duty power tool which isn't all that vital for the average home renovator to own.

Most standard saber saws come with four blades—the one with the largest teeth is for rough wood cuts, the medium ones are for smoother wood cuts and sheetrock, and the finest one is for metal work.

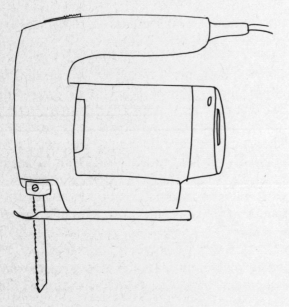

saber saw

HANDY ADDITIONS

Wood Chisel

We had to pick up a wood chisel for the first time the day we were forced to learn the frustrating job of setting hinges into a door. Wood chisels are very simple tools, but they're not simple to manipulate skillfully. They come in many shapes and sizes, and their basic function is to cut out or carve wood. We've gotten along so far with just one ¾" tang chisel. If you're going to invest in a second one, a ¼" is the most useful.

Notice that the working end is beveled, which means tapered, to enable the tool to cut cleanly into the wood. It must be sharp to be of any use. Hold the beveled edge against the wood when you're roughing out a cut, and move the chisel along by striking the metal cap on top of the handle with your hammer. To smooth the cut, place the flat (back) side against the wood, but this time produce forward pressure with your hand rather than with a striking tool.

In addition to setting hinges into a door, you can use your chisel to remove an old, damaged floorboard or to unstick a window jammed closed with dry paint.

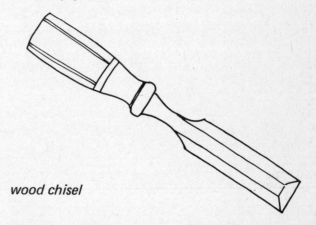

wood chisel

Plane

A plane is much like a wood chisel blade that's set into a metal housing, allowing the user to shave the wood surface flat and smooth. The plane has come into our lives only twice so far: once when we had to reshape a window sash that wasn't moving up and down easily, and again to trim a bathroom door after we put in a new tile floor.

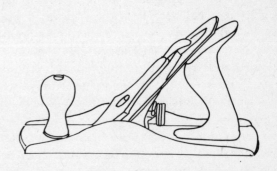

plane

Vise

Vises and clamps were invented to relieve you of the awkwardness of trying to hold a piece of wood or metal steady while you're drilling, gluing, sanding, or planing it. A portable woodworking vise whose jaws open to a maximum of three inches is the smartest choice. First secure the clamp base to your workbench. Open the jaws wide enough to admit the work, and then close them again to lock it firmly in place.

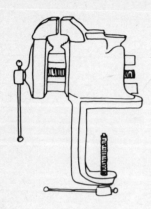

vise

Miter Box

A miter is an angled cut (usually 45°) sawed at the ends of two pieces of wood (or any other material) which are to be joined at a corner. The miter box pictured here is designed to enable you to make such cuts accurately. Most of the time, you'll be using it with various kinds of wood trim—moldings, quarter round, baseboards, etc. It's best to buy one with relatively high sides so that you can cut both larger and smaller pieces of lumber. The best saw for the job is a special kind of crosscut saw called a *backsaw*, which has very closely spaced teeth to insure extreme precision and a heavy metal "spine" over the blade to keep the tool cutting along an absolutely straight line. The backsaw should be held horizontal to the wood surface instead of at an angle as with the crosscut and ripsaw.

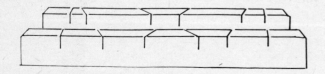

miter box

Prybar, Flatbar, Crowbar

A prybar will handle any number of operations, many, though not all of them, connected with the removal of unwanted materials: pulling baseboard or ceiling moldings away from the walls, taking up old floor tiles, or prying up large nails. You simply wedge the end of the bar beneath whatever it is you want to remove, and use the tool as a lever to work it loose.

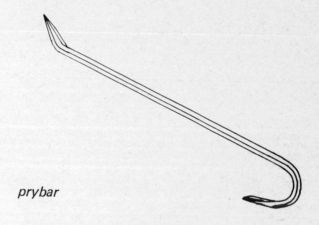

prybar

Propane Torch, Blow Torch

An efficient tool for removing paint which eliminates the torture of applying and scraping off three or more applications of liquid paint remover. It consists of a small replaceable tank filled with inflammable propane. By turning a valve you release a thin stream of the gas through the attached tip; ignite it with a match and apply the flame to the painted surface. Within seconds, the old layers of paint—no matter how many there are—blister and can be worked loose with a 3" scraping knife. Obviously, you don't want to operate this tool without observing the strictest safety percautions, but with the proper care, you needn't be afraid of it.

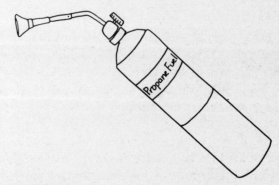

propane torch

Sharpening Stones

Almost everyone knows that tools need sharpening occasionally; the problem is being either too forgetful or too lazy to do it. Dull tools are not only inefficient but hazardous. You can take almost any tool to a hardware store to be sharpened for small change. Certainly with a saw or a drill bit, that's the right place to go. But for chisels, small knives, utility scissors, and the like, a sharpening stone is worth owning. Get a long rectangular one with a handle and, preferably, both a coarse and a smooth sharpening surface.

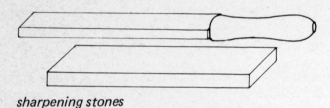

sharpening stones

STANDARD HARDWARE

This illustrated guide includes only the most fundamental hardware—things worth having on hand at all times. It's a good idea to pick up what's called a workshop organizer, one of those upright, rectangular metal boxes with many small plastic drawers for storing nuts, bolts, screws, hooks, nails, and other small items.

Common Nails, Flat Head Nails

For all-purpose wood construction flat head nails are used. The galvanized common nails are best because they have added holding power. Graduated sizes are indicated by a number (not a reference to inches) followed by the letter *d* (translated as "penny"). Thus 2d is called "two penny" (1 inch long), 3d is "three penny" (1¼" long), and so on up to 20d (4 inches long).

Finishing Nails

Finishing nails are designed so the heads can be driven just below the surface and hidden from view. You would use them whenever you don't want nailheads to show. Size designations are exactly the same as for common nails.

Brads

Tiny finishing nails often used to attach thin moldings to furniture or to secure a picture inside its frame are called brads.

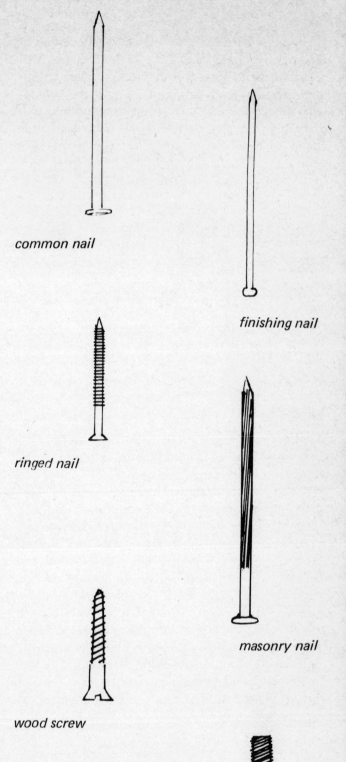

common nail

finishing nail

ringed nail

masonry nail

wood screw

nut   *bolt*

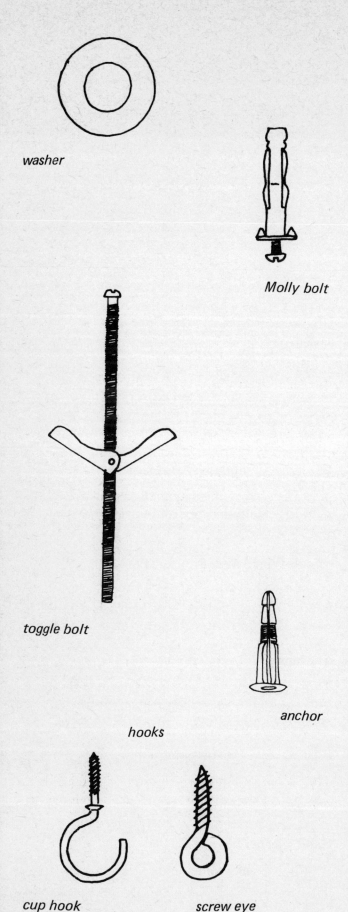

washer

Molly bolt

toggle bolt

anchor

hooks

cup hook   *screw eye*

Spikes

Common nails larger than four inches are spikes. Usually not identified by "d" but by size in inches.

Sheetrock Nails, Blue Nails

These are 1¼", 1⅜", 1½" long nails with a blue-black finish made for attaching sheetrock to studs in the wall. You can buy them with ringed shanks, for extra gripping power—on the ceiling, for example, or smooth ones.

Masonry Nails, Cut Nails

A special nail that can be driven directly into a concrete, stone, brick, or mortar surface, usually when you want to hang something decorative is a masonry nail. The notched one holds more firmly, but both kinds need to be hammered in slowly and with patience.

Ringed Nails, Annular Nails

To secure plywood to the permanent flooring when preparing a subfloor for tiling, use ring nails.

Wood Screws

They are used to attach things to studs (the vertical 2' x 3's or 2' x 4's inside your wall), to fasten two pieces of wood together, or driven into anchors (plugs) to fasten objects to a hollow wall. Its threads allow for greater holding strength than the nail, and of course it can be removed and reset more easily. Make sure you select the right size screwdriver. Note, too, that Phillips screws can be driven only with a Phillips screwdriver.

Bolts

These allow for still greater holding power than screws or nails. The threaded shank, instead of biting into the wood fibers, is secured with a nut at one end which holds tightly against the surface.

Washers

Circular metal or rubber discs with a hole in the middle are washers. The metal ones are used between a nut and a piece of wood to prevent marring of the surface, or between the bolt head and the wood to keep the head from slipping through the hole. The rubber ones are used in plumbing to hold back water seepage.

Molly Bolt, Hollow Wall Anchor

This is a device for fastening a light-to-medium-weight object to a hollow wall faced with plaster or sheetrock. Once installed, the metal strips which make up the shield expand and grip the wall from behind. The most common size to buy is ¼".

Toggle Bolt, Butterfly

It is used to attach medium-weight objects to a hollow wall or ceiling faced with plaster or sheetrock, or to cinder block, concrete block, or hollow tile walls as well.

Anchors, Plugs, Shields

These are small bullet-shaped casings which you tap into a wall after drilling a hole. The presence of an anchor provides a solid grip for your screw, which you can then insert to hold up light-to-medium-weight objects.

Plastic anchors are for fastening lightweight objects to a hollow plaster or sheetrock wall.

Lead anchors are for fastening medium-to-heavyweight objects to a masonry wall (concrete, brick, etc.).

Hooks

For loose hanging of light objects, several kinds of hooks are used. A cup hook is for cups, small plants, or decorative items.

A screw eye or eye hook is to hang items that already have hooks on them, or to put on either side of a painting for attaching picture-hanging wire.

STAPLES FOR THE WORK AREA

Joint Compound, Spackle

A plasterlike substance used to repair small cracks in a plaster or sheetrock wall is called spackle. It is also applied to the tape which covers the seams in butted pieces of sheetrock. Its chief advantage is that it takes a little more time to harden than plaster of Paris and can thus be worked somewhat longer. Available either in powder or premixed (vinyl spackle) form.

Patching Plaster

This is used to repair larger cracks and holes in a plaster wall. It consists of plaster of Paris to which a retardant compound has been added. This slows down the drying time somewhat and gives you some leeway for spreading and smoothing the mixture.

Cement

A sand mix is a compound of powdered limestone and clay used for covering floors and repairing small holes in concrete.

Concrete

Cement to which small stones have been added becomes concrete. Used for paving walks, patios, and driveways.

Putty

A thick substance, the texture of soft clay, used to secure a pane of glass to a window sash, it is also called glazing compound.

Caulking Compound

This is an aid in insulation, used with a caulking gun, to seal up the crevices between window and frame.

Plastic Wood, Wood Putty, Wood Filler

It is a paste-like compound which can be spread over cracks, gouges, or spaces in wood to fill in the gaps. Don't use it to cover large areas.

Machine Oil

This oil is used as a lubricant and rust inhibitor for saws and other tools (where appropriate). Use sparingly! And always wipe off the excess.

Rust Remover, Penetrating Oil

This is a thick liquid which can be applied to garden tools, steel windows, saws, etc. to remove accumulated rust.

Hand Cleaner

A thick jelly-like compound for heavy duty cleaning of the hands after a long day of work, it is excellent to have around.

Rubber Gloves

It is advisable to wear them when you are working with paint remover or any other highly corrosive chemical.

Creosote

A chemical which you can brush over outdoor wood surfaces to protect them from the deteriorating effects of the weather, creosote gives the wood a rich, brown tone that obviates the need for any other kind of stain or finish.

Electrical Tape

Wrap this tape around exposed electrical connections to insulate the wire and prevent the hazard of shock.

Glue

The epoxy glues are good for joining pieces of wood, but to form a solid bond, you must clamp the surfaces together after application. Good for repairing window sash frames, furniture joints, and even (when mixed with sawdust) building up cracks and gouges in damaged floorboards.

Contact cement, although somewhat less permanent than epoxy, has many uses: to mend china and wood objects, to apply formica to a kitchen work surface, to attach a fixture on bathroom ceramic tile. It does not require clamping.

In general, don't apply glue when you can use a nail, screw, bolt, or other more permanent fastener.

As to the miracle glues now flooding the market, we have used them with only middling success. Proceed at your own risk.

Sandpaper

Paper coated with abrasive sand and used to smooth wood surfaces and to remove chipped paint or scratches is called sandpaper.

Steel Wool

Like sandpaper, steel wool is used as an abrasive on wood or metal. It is available in grades ranging from 0000 (extra fine) to 3 (coarse). Use to remove wax from a soiled floor, smooth wood between applications of finishing material, and, especially,

to remove old paint after applying liquid paint remover.

Wire Brush

A wire brush is handy for any number of odd cleaning jobs.

Toothbrush

It is just about the only thing to use for working into hard-to-reach notches, grooves, and corners when you are staining a wood floor or cleaning a surface prior to painting.

Mineral Spirits, Turpentine, Benzine, Brush Cleaner, Paint Thinner

Liquid petroleum derivatives are used to clean up brushes after painting, to loosen dried paint from old brushes, to thin oil-based paints, varnishes, etc.

Lacquer Thinner

To thin the spreading consistency of lacquer, it is also a solvent for certain brands of plastic wood.

Acetone

It is a solvent for certain glues.

Paint Remover

This is a strongly corrosive liquid chemical for removing paint from a wood or metal surface. The paint must generally be given several applications and then worked loose with a metal scraper and steel wool.

Denatured Alcohol

It is used for thinning shellac.

Stain

A pigment usually containing a penetrating sealer which you apply to a wood floor or piece of furniture to give it heightened color and bring out the natural grain is called a stain.

Bleach

Plain laundry bleach can lighten wood tone the same way stain can darken it.

Wood Finish

A liquid which you brush on wood to give it a protective coating and enriched lustre, examples are shellac, varnish, polyurethane.

Sash Chain

Chain used along with a weight, pulley, and accompanying hardware to facilitate the opening and closing of window sash.

Ladder

Available in either aluminum or wood, the metal ones are good for indoor use only, while the wooden ones can be used both indoors and outdoors. Buy one with a minimum 250 rating; a cheap ladder will be hazardous in the long run.

BASIC CARPENTRY SKILLS

How to Drive a Nail

If, like us, you have somehow passed into adulthood without being able to wield a hammer with some degree of authority, then hide yourself in a dark corner of the basement, set up some scrap wood, and begin practicing. A beginner's instinct usually leads him to choke up on the handle. This is a mistake, since it cuts down on leverage and reduces the force of the blow.

1.) Grasp the handle at the end, and, using your free hand to support the nail, gently tap it into the surface so that it rests at a *slight* angle to the wood. (It's not really desirable to hit the nail perfectly straight.)

2.) Remove your inactive hand to a safe distance.

3.) Aiming squarely for the center of the nailhead, strike it repeatedly until it lies flat on the wood.

4.) To *countersink* a finishing nail—which means to drive its small head slightly below the surface so as to hide it from view—place a nailset on the head, tap it in just a bit farther, and fill the hole with plastic wood. Don't try to hammer a nail in too close to the edge of a board. You'll simply chip the wood and have to start again.

How to Remove a Nail

This is where the claw end of the hammer comes in.

1.) Raise the nailhead slightly above the wood surface by prying it up with a screwdriver, grasping it with a pliers, or digging it up with a handy device called a "cat's claw."

2.) Set the claw end of the hammer under the nailhead and pull the nail free. A helpful trick is to wedge a small block of wood under the hammer head to allow for a neater extraction. Also, if you simply can't get hold of the nailhead because it's too deeply imbedded, leave it in and use a nailset to countersink it still further, then woodfill the hole.

How to Drive a Screw

Many beginners wrongly assume that you start to drive a screw by setting it against a wood surface, inserting the screwdriver blade, and turning clockwise. This can be a frustrating way to learn. You grunt as you rotate the screw for five minutes, and still the thread doesn't catch the wood.

There is a simple remedy:

Make a starter hole with either a drill or threaded awl (the awl is for relatively small holes that you want to bore manually, but a nail or a nailpunch can make larger starter holes when needed). Regardless of the tool you use, make sure to select one that will give you a hole slightly deeper and narrower than the dimensions of the screw, or you'll find the threads gripping the air.

After making the starter hole you can now easily insert the screw.

One agonizing moment occurs when all your strength fails to turn a partially driven screw. This is not the time to struggle onward or to attack the head with a hammer which may split the wood. Just remove the screw, bore a *slightly* wider staring hole, and try again.

A bar of soap rubbed against the threads of a screw will help you sink it in much the same as it eases the removal of a tight ring from a finger.

A special problem sometimes develops when screws are inserted and removed from the same surfaces repeatedly over a period of years. The holes become gradually larger, and there is no longer anything for the screw threads to hold onto. Larger screws only aggravate the situation since a few years later, still larger ones will be needed. A handy old carpenter's remedy is to cut up a toothpick, and place the small bits of wood into the hole so that the threads of the same size screws will again have something to bite into.

If you are screwing into a free-standing surface, such as an unattached board, use a vise.

How to Remove a Screw

Screws are usually more cooperative about coming out than going in. You select the right screwdriver, set in the blade, and turn counter-clockwise. When they decide to be stubborn, though, there are three possible cures:

1.) Chip away any old paint that was clogging the slot and try again.

2.) Sometimes, with a bit of maneuvering, you can grab the sides of the head with a pliers, and start the counter-clockwise motion going.

3.) Try the brace and bit. It has screwdriver attachments that fit it and the further advantage of a reversible ratchet that will give you more twisting power than the screwdriver.

How to Saw Across a Piece of Lumber Against the Grain

Using a saw for the first time can be very discouraging. It is one of those acts of coordination one learns better from watching and doing than from a set of printed directions. The steps listed below, however, can serve as a practical guide.

The most common mistake is to assume that it's all a matter of brute strength. To the contrary, if your wood is properly braced, and the saw is well sharpened and cared for, sheer force will impede rather than aid you.

1.) Use the crosscut saw.

2.) Check to see that it is well sharpened by running your index finger lightly across the blade.

3.) Apply a thin coat of machine oil to the entire blade, and then wipe off the excess. This lubrication will prevent the blade from binding (catching) and make your work easier.

4.) Measure the length of board to be cut away by making dots with a pencil at equivalent points along both edges and connect them. This is your guideline.

5.) If you can conveniently set the board to be cut in a vise, do so. You want to avoid allowing the wood to slip around while it's being sawed. If

this isn't possible, then lay the wood flat on your workbench or sawhorse, and position it so that the section to be cut lies over the edge.

6.) Pick up the saw and set the blade straight (not at an angle) over the penciled line. Using your free hand, brace the board.

7.) Move the saw *easily* back and forth over the line until the teeth begin to bite into the wood. This gives you the important starting line that will prevent the saw from moving off course later on.

8.) Now set the blade in the far side of the groove and tilt it in at a 45° angle. Stroke evenly back and forth, gradually increasing the length of the strokes and keeping your free hand in place as a guide. Use the whole blade, not just the middle portion. Also keep the sawing arm steady and free, away from your body and the working surface.

9.) Follow the guideline all the way across. When you come to the end, slow down, and, supporting the side to be cut away with your free hand, gently detach the wood.

Snags can crop up at any time. For the beginner, the following are common:

The strokes become more and more difficult as you go along, until you finally can't budge the saw at all. The blade is probably getting bound up in the saw cut itself. Try applying greater downward pressure with your free hand on the waste end of the board to prevent binding.

The saw keeps moving off course. In your anxiety to see that the blade is doing its job well, you're watching the saw rather than the pencil mark. Twist the handle in the opposite direction just a bit, and with a few more easy strokes, you should be back on track. Keep your eye on the guideline this time.

The blade is cutting at an angle rather than directly perpendicular to the wood surface so that eventually the saw slows to a halt. You're working too hard and forcing the blade. The only sane solution is to start again.

You're doing everything right, but the process is slow and agonizing. This either means that the blade is duller than you thought or that your wood is too damp. It's useless to go ahead until either or both of these conditions are corrected.

To Saw the Length of a Piece of Wood with the Grain

Use the ripsaw. The technique is the same except

that once the blade has established itself in the guideline, it should be tilted at an angle somewhat closer to vertical than with the crosscut saw (about 60°).

As with the process of crosscutting, you may find the blade binding as you go along. Place a small wedge into the already cut portion to keep the space sufficiently wide.

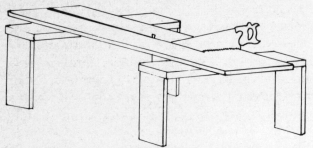

How to Operate the Saber Saw

1.) First secure the blade by loosening a screw at the front, inserting the blade with the teeth pointing out, and tightening the screw firmly. These blades have been known to work loose under heavy pressure.

2.) Notice that the teeth of the blade point upward, meaning that it does its cutting on the "up" stroke. For that reason, if your wood has both a smooth side and a rough side, place the smooth side *down* on the workbench, and then the surface that is already rough can be the one that gets slightly splintered from the cutting action of the blade.

3.) Measure and mark the material.

4.) The flat plate that extends in front of and behind the blade is called "the shoe." Turn the saber saw on (if it is a variable speed model, you will probably find the faster rpm more efficient), and lower the shoe flat onto the starting edge of the material.

5.) Inch the saw forward slowly until the blade comes into contact with the penciled guideline.

6.) Continue to push ahead, following the line and not looking at the blade.

7.) As with manual sawing, you must be careful near the end of a cut to brace the material so that it doesn't splinter off.

It's important not to be impatient with the blade. The saber saw isn't designed to do particularly fast cutting, so forcing it ahead will only overheat the machine. After awhile, you'll develop a feel for how much pressure can safely be applied.

One of those obvious but crucial safety warnings: Don't put your fingers in a position where the blade can get at them. Of all power tools, the electic saw needs to be treated with the highest degree of caution.

Since the action of the saber saw blade is reciprocating, meaning that it has a back and forth motion, you can't simply set the machine in the center of a piece of wood to make an internal cut—for example, to cut a rectangle into a piece of paneling for a light switch. The blade will just knock against the surface with a nasty smack. Instead, *drill* a big enough hole inside the area to be cut away so that you can now insert the saw blade and approach the penciled guideline from within. Some machines enable you to apply a technique called "piercing," whereby you can gradually tilt the saber saw in at an angle and begin an internal cut without first using the drill. This isn't as easy as it sounds, however, so study the accompanying manual carefully before you try it.

How to Drill a Hole into Wood, Sheetrock, or Plaster

Although someday you may have to drill into a hard material like brick, most of the time, you'll be using this tool on the walls, and that generally means wood, sheetrock, or plaster. Let's suppose you're drilling a relatively small hole into your wall.

1.) Use an awl and hammer to mark the precise spot where you want the bit to penetrate. This starter hole will keep the bit from slipping off course.

2.) Select the proper high speed steel bit. The right choice can be a matter of using your eye, but sometimes the directions for whatever job you're doing will specify a definite size. If you do err, it's better to make a hole that's too small than one that's too large.

3.) Your drill comes with a chuck key that has a playful way of walking off. It's best to tie it to the power cord the second you open the box. Take the key, and insert it into the chuck, opening the jaws enough so that they will accept the shank of the size bit you have selected. Now reverse the movement so that the jaws lock the bit in good and tight. Remove the key from the chuck before you start work.

4.) Position the tip of the bit directly in the

starter hole, holding it perpendicular to the material.

5.) Squeeze the trigger to activate the drill. If it's a variable speed machine, begin at low speed, and as you exert forward pressure, switch to higher speed. Don't tilt the angle of the drill. All that will do is strain the motor and cause the bit to get stuck in the surface.

6.) As soon as the bit no longer meets resistance, the drill has finished boring the hole. Withdraw it WITH THE POWER STILL ON. Don't try to remove it after you have released the trigger.

Special Situations

You are guiding the bit smoothly forward when suddenly it comes up against a surface that feels like the facade of a steel vault. Don't push ahead. You're probably up against an outside solid wall, one usually made of concrete, concrete block, or cinder block. All this means is that you need a special drill bit for masonry.

masonry bit

For drilling larger holes into wood, a special set of bits called spade bits are used. You'll need these for a job like installing locks. Our set ranges in diameter from ⅜'' up to 1⅜''. It's wise to begin with a starter hole for these, since the relatively large diameter of the bit makes it easy for the tip to run off course.

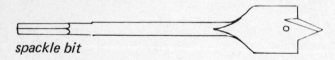

spackle bit

Anytime a piece of material to be drilled is small enough to hold in the hand, it should be set up at your workbench and well secured with a vise or clamp. It's impossible to get anything like an accurate cut with the wood flipping around.

An added tip when working with wood is to place a small piece of scrap lumber *under* the board you're drilling to prevent splintering.

Power drills today can be fitted with a staggering array of fancy attachments, enough to fill the rest of this chapter: buffers, sanders, grinding wheels, wire brushes. They are unevenly effective, however, especially the screwdriver bits.

How to Power Sand a Surface

The directions below are for the use of the kind of power finishing sander described earlier in this chapter. There may be certain jobs for which it is unsuited, refinishing a floor, for example, but if you are going to own any kind of power sander this is the most versatile.

1.) Buy a supply of either garnet (orange) or aluminum oxide (red) sandpaper in each of three grades—coarse, medium, fine. For especially rough jobs you may need extra coarse, and for especially smooth jobs, extra fine, but most of the time the three standard grades will suffice. Stay away from the cheaper *flint* paper. It does a decent job for about four minutes, and then it's ready to be thrown away. Most jobs, especially removing gouges and nicks from woodwork, will require that you begin with a coarse (maybe even extra coarse) grade and gradually work down to medium and fine.

2.) Take a utility scissors and cut the sheet so that it will fit neatly over the pad at the bottom of the sander, remembering that there must be about a ½'' overlap at both ends to secure the paper to the machine. For ours, 3⅝'' x 9'' is perfect.

3.) Some finishing sander models have levers at either end with which to attach the paper, but the newer ones generally use paper clamps. These can be a little awkward to work with, but once the paper is secured with the help of a screwdriver, they hold very effectively. The manufacturer certainly didn't design things this way, but we've found that the only effective technique for installing the paper is to hold the machine between your legs with the pad facing you. MAKE SURE THE PLUG IS OUT. Take the screwdriver in one hand, and wedge it into the small opening in the center of the clamp. Now tilt the screwdriver back slightly so that the clamp opens a little. With your free hand, grab the piece of sandpaper. Insert one end evenly into the slot about ½''; then release the screwdriver. Crease the paper over the pad, turn the sander around, and repeat the process, bending the other end over the side and under the second clamp with a screwdriver. It should lie flat and be evenly centered.

4.) Plug in the machine, but first make sure that the power switch is "off." If you're working some distance from the power source, check the owner's manual that comes with your machine for information about the proper gauge extension cord to use.

5.) Holding the sander just above the work surface, turn the switch on, and gently lower the paper to contact with the wood.

6.) Move the sander easily back and forth over the surface. You'll be working with the grain of the wood most of the time, but there's no reason why you can't sand across it here and there.

Don't overtax the machine. If you feel it overheating, stop and find out the cause.

Don't become too attached to one piece of paper. As soon as you find your efficiency reduced by a worn strip, stop and replace it. Of course, this shouldn't be happening every two and a half minutes.

You'll find it necessary to tilt the sander at an angle (sometimes at quite an extreme angle) in order to get close to a narrow edge, a bulge, or a curve. The operating instructions won't tell you to do this, but there is no way of avoiding it. The only thing to watch out for here is placing undue pressure on the front or back edges of the sandpaper strip for it will promptly rip.

How to Plane a Wood Surface

1.) Clamp or brace the work if possible.

2.) Rotate the adjusting nut of the plane to allow the blade to protrude enough for the depth of cut you want.

3.) Glide it evenly over the surface of the wood.

As easy as this sounds, there are a lot of ways you can go wrong.

Don't plane against the grain. If you do, the blade will catch in the wood, producing a succession of dents and ripples—exactly the opposite result of what you want.

Don't use a small plane against the edge of a long board. You'll wind up with a series of hills and dales instead of a flat straight line. The "jack plane," about 14" long, is probably the most versatile you can buy. If you don't anticipate doing too much heavy work, though, any of the conveniently sized "smoothing planes" will do.

Don't begin or end a cut with the plane held at an angle to the wood. Keep it as nearly parallel as possible.

Don't allow wood shavings to get stuck in the mouth of the blade. These will have a similar effect on the tool's efficiency as does skin that continually gets caught in the blade of a potato peeler.

Chapter 5

Walls, Ceilings, and Windows

WALLS: BASIC STRUCTURE

We're not going to show you how to demolish and build partitions in your house because that work demands pretty sophisticated carpentry skills. You should, however, know enough about your walls to understand at least something about how they're constructed; otherwise anything you try to hang on them is likely to end up on the floor.

Let's start with three fundamental principles:

Some of your walls help support the structure of the house; others simply divide the interior space.

There is something *behind* the wall other than air. You can't do anything to a wall before you know what that something is.

The visible surface of a wall can be made of any number of possible materials (wood, wood paneling, brick), but the most common are plaster and sheetrock.

The distinction between bearing and non-bearing isn't all that important to make, unless you plan to tear a wall down. If you do, you're obviously going to have to know which is which because demolishing a bearing wall can be hazardous to the health of your house. They are most often *exterior* walls (their opposite side is actually the outside of the house). Non-bearing walls, on the other hand, are most often *interior* walls (they just serve as partitions for the rooms inside the house). So if you tear apart one of these, you won't be bringing down a section of the roof along with it. Like most generalizations, this one has its exceptions, so don't take a sledge hammer to any wall unless you know exactly what you're up against.

What you *are* up against can be better under-stood if you approach a given wall at random and knock against it with your fist (not too hard!). If the sound you make is a dense, heavy thump, you're probably hitting a *solid* wall—usually an exterior, bearing wall constructed of concrete, concrete block, or brick. If the sound you make is lighter or more open, you are probably tapping a *hollow* wall—usually an interior, non-bearing wall constructed of a network of vertical boards called studs to which the visible outside surface has been applied.

That leaves us with the visible outer surface. The original walls in an old house are probably of plaster, several layers of which are applied to the wall over a framework of lath—thin wood strips nailed horizontally to the studs, or metal mesh similarly attached. Newer houses usually have sheetrock walls—those familiar 4' x 8' rectangles of gypsum plaster sandwiched between thick layers of paper. It comes in ⅜", ½", and ⅝" thicknesses, the first two being the most common-ly used.

It's unfortunate, but there's no way to see through this outer surface unless you have x-ray vision. The best you can do is to drill into some hidden corner and observe carefully the qualities of the dust you get and the degree of resistance that the drill bit meets. More about this in the next section.

WALLS: FASTENINGS

The first do-it-yourself project we successfully executed was to tap a picture hook into one of our apartment walls and hang a newly bought painting. We were proud, indeed, not to have had to hire a contractor to do the job. Although not every wall fastening operation is as elementary, you can do much to simplify your work if you consider each of the following questions in logical sequence:

What material is the surface of the wall made of, and what lies behind it?

How heavy is the object you want to attach?

Does the object hang from the wall (like a picture), or is it secured to it (like a shelf)?

What you'd like most to be able to do with any object you need to hang on the wall is just to hammer it in with a few nails, or attach it to a picture hook. With a light painting or mirror, you can probably get away with that. But as soon as the weight increases, you're going to have to select another more suitable fastener in order to get a solid grip on the wall.

The interior structure of the wall is your most important determinant here. How do you find out what that structure is, assuming you don't already know? Here's where the drill test comes in.

Take any moderate size bit, fit it into the chuck, and position the machine in front of a well-obscured section of the wall—some area, for example, behind a cabinet or dresser. Then allow the bit to penetrate the wall as far as it will go. The dust fallout that results from this probe will give you valuable clues as to what lies within:

If You Get . . .	You Probably Have . . .
white powder, then empty space	hollow plaster or sheetrock wall
white powder, then wood shavings	hollow plaster or sheetrock wall—you've located one of the studs
white powder, then brown powder, then empty space	hollow plaster wall with a brown undercoating
white powder, then hard going	solid wall—the dust that spills out should either be light gray (indicating concrete) or red (indicating brick)

There are many other possibilities and combinations, but these are by far the most common ones.

Here's how to proceed. If you've just determined that your wall is *solid*—concrete, filled concrete block, or brick—you're going to have a harder time attaching anything to it, regardless of whether the facing material is plaster or sheetrock. But if the wall is *hollow*—studs faced with plaster or sheetrock—the going should be reasonably smooth, so let's start there.

Hollow Walls

Picture in your mind the space that lies inside a hollow wall. What you have are vertical strips of wood (the studs) hopefully spaced at regular 16" or 24" intervals and covered over with lath and plaster or sheetrock. For the best hold, here's a rule worth remembering:

Objects obstened to a wall should, whenever possible, be attached to studs.

Thus, if you want to put up a medium-weight or heavy object, merely attach the object by setting an appropriate sized screw, nail, or hook into the stud. To do this, you should first put a small piece of transparent Scotch tape on the wall to prevent chipping, make a starter hole with your awl, and drive the nail or screw right through the layer of plaster and into the wood.

Short of tearing down the outer wall, we have found no foolproof method to figure out where those studs are. Here are some possibilities.

How to Locate the Studs in a Hollow Wall

1.) Tap your hand along the surface. When the studs come up, you'll get a more solid thud. Personally, we have never been able to tell the difference.

2.) Buy a device called a *stud finder* at your hardware store. Beware, though. This gadget promises more than it delivers, and its mini-magnet is often inaccurate.

3.) The only fully reliable method, but a sloppy one: hammer a small nail into the wall in places you know will later be hidden from view. Of course, you can always use a bit of spackle to repair these later on if you like.

Plastic Anchors

You've probably already figured out, though, that the occasions where it is convenient to nail into a stud are relatively few. Enter the plastic anchor, called variously a plastic shield or plug. These are fairly small, bulletlike structures with notched sides which you will use for mounting light-to-medium-weight objects to a hollow wall, *whenever a stud doesn't lie behind the point of attachment*. Since a screw won't hold by itself, you insert one of these anchors into the wall, and drive the screw into *it* instead. As the screw shank penetrates the wall, it forces the sides of the anchor to expand and hence bite into and grip the surrounding plaster. Here's the whole process, using a small wooden display cabinet (like a medicine chest) for illustrative purposes. It's not essential, but definitely helpful, for two people to work together on this.

How to Install a Plastic Anchor

1.) Get the approximate weight of your cabinet, then buy the appropriate size plastic anchors and corresponding screws to hold it (they're usually sold together).

2.) Locate the exact spot where you want to position the cabinet, and make a pencil mark right in the center of your attachment points (places on the object where the screws will go). If you plan to drill holes through the back of the cabinet to accept the screws because there isn't any attachment hardware, place them far enough apart so that the unit will be well supported. Use a level to make certain that the pencil marks form a true horizontal.

3.) Begin at any of the corners by tapping a tiny hole into one of the pencil markings with your awl.

4.) Take either a power drill or a brace and bit, and fit the chuck with the right size bit for setting the anchor in the wall. This information is usually printed on the package. If it's not, you'll have to use your eye. The hole should be just big enough to accept the tip of the anchor without allowing the other end to sink back and disappear into the wall.

5.) Position your bit on the starter hole and drill through.

6.) Take the anchor in hand and lightly hit it with a hammer until it lies flat in the wall.

7.) Continue in exactly this way to sink the remaining anchors *before you attempt to mount the cabinet.*

8.) At this point, an extra pair of hands is welcome. One person can hold the cabinet steady, while the other drives the screws through the attachment points on the cabinet and into the anchors.

Molly Bolts

Since plastic anchors cannot sustain too much weight, for medium-weight objects, you'll have to graduate to a device called a *hollow wall fastener* (more popularly, the Molly bolt). It's just a more sophisticated anchor consisting of a metal casing (shield) and a bolt that screws into the casing. Once you've drilled a hole and inserted the casing into the wall, the bolt is screwed in, and as it turns, the casing itself pulls back, opens up, and grips the wall from behind. The result is an extremely secure fastening which binds from both the front and the back simultaneously. We'll demonstrate the process this time using a medium-weight shelf unit (1' x 3') as our example.

How to Install a Molly Bolt

1.) Get the approximate weight of your shelf, taking into account how light or heavy a load it's going to have to support. In most instances, you'll be able to use ¼" Mollies.

2.) Correctly screw the brackets into the shelf.

3.) Locate the exact spot where you want to position the shelf and place a level over it to make sure it's perfectly horizontal. Holding the shelf in place with one hand, take your pencil in the other, and make a mark right in the center of the places where the screws will go. Set the shelf aside.

4.) Begin by tapping a tiny hole into either one of the pencil markings with your awl.

5.) Take a power drill or brace and bit, and fit the chuck with the right size bit to accommodate the Molly in the wall. If it's a ¼" Molly, you use a ¼" bit, and so on.

6.) Position the bit on the starter hole and drill through.

7.) Remove the bolt from the Molly, and gently tap the casing flat against the wall. Notice that there are two small metal notches behind the opening. These serve an important purpose. You want to hammer the casing in so that these sharp "teeth" dig into the plaster. They will keep the unit from rotating while you screw in the bolt.

8.) Now slowly begin screwing in the bolt. This will take a bit of time and pressure because the metal strips are pulling back against the inside of the wall as you turn.

9.) When the bolt refuses to go in any further, it means that the Molly is properly positioned. Reverse the direction of your screwdriver and pull the bolt out again.

10.) Repeat the process with the remaining

Molly (or Mollies).

11.) Hold the shelf bracket in position over the appropriate holes, set the bolts in one at a time, and screw them clockwise to tighten.

Toggle Bolts

Some years ago when we landed an astonishing bargain on an antique kitchen cabinet known as a Hoosier, we got the bright idea of detaching the upper section (a 12″ x 21″ x 42″ rectangle) and hanging it on a hollow wall suspended by decorative chain. This is just the sort of instance where Mollies aren't quite up to the job, and you'll need to use toggle bolts instead. The reason isn't just that toggle bolts can support more weight, but that they are just the thing to hold up objects lying against the wall as opposed to hanging from it. Like the Molly, they grip the wall from both front and back, but they are constructed somewhat differently. The toggle consists of a bolt and an attached nut to which are connected two "wings." These can be folded down so that when the unit is pushed through a hole the wings spring open and are drawn back against the wall to lock tight. It takes a bit more finesse to install them than it does the Molly, but we'll take the procedure slowly, step by step, using the Hoosier cabinet as our example. Four hands are most definitely advised!

How to Install a Toggle Bolt

1.) Take the approximate weight of your cabinet, and buy the appropriate size toggle bolts to hold it (ask your dealer for advice). Remember to take into account the added weight of whatever the cabinet will be holding.

2.) Locate the exact spot where you want to position the cabinet; then either hold it against the wall while someone else traces the perimeter with a pencil, or simply take down the dimensions and transfer them to the wall without holding up the cabinet. In any case, be sure to use a level to check for true horizontal.

3.) Choose the two points where the toggle bolts will be installed. They should be spaced equally near the top and an inch or two in from the sides. Mark them with a pencil, and tap in a small starter hole with your awl.

4.) You're now ready for the drilling. The hole you drill needs to be a relatively wide one since

you've got to make it big enough so that not just the bolt but the folded wings, as well, can push through to the other side of the wall. Notice the number on the toggle. It's a measure of the thickness of the bolt, *not* of this first hole that you'll be drilling. You want a hold exactly twice as big as that thickness, so choose the appropriate bit, and fit it into the chuck.

The toggle is quite a bit longer than a plastic anchor or Molly, and that's where the complications can crop up. You need enough hollow space back there to fit the full length of the bolt. Usually, you'll have all you need. But if this particular hollow wall is concrete block with plaster or sheetrock facing, you may find your drill meeting fierce resistance once you get through the outer surface. Here's all you need to do if this is the case: move the drill an inch or so in and down, and drill through again. This time, with good fortune, you will find yourself positioned over one of the inside holes in the block and home free.

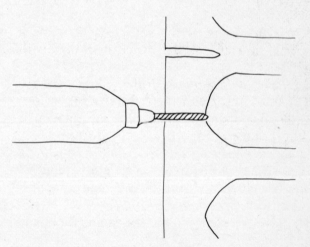

drilling through concrete block

5.) Now that you've drilled the holes in the wall, you're ready for the cabinet. There is only one right way to do this, so follow it carefully:

Measure the *exact* distance from the top penciled line on the wall to the *center* of the left hole you've drilled, and then from the left vertical penciled line to the center of the same hole. Now transfer these dimensions onto the back surface of the cabinet. You should have a point where the lines meet. Do the same on the right side.

6.) Fit your drill this time with a bit whose size corresponds to the thickness of the *bolt* (not the toggle)—that's the number printed on the wing. In

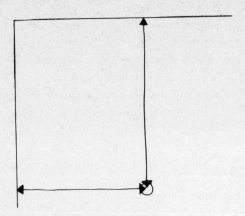

markings for hanging the cabinets

other words, you're going to bore holes in the cabinet half as large as the ones you put in the wall so that the bolt heads will hold the cabinet securely. Drill these holes through the center of the dots you drew in step 5).

7.) Remove the toggle nuts from the bolts. Put the bolts through the two holes you've just drilled into the cabinet, attaching the nuts with the wing flaps pointed towards you. Now rotate them a few turns. That's right. The bolts must be attached to the object BEFORE you lift it onto the wall.

8.) Here's the tricky part. One person will have to hold the cabinet steady against the wall while the other firms up the toggle bolts. Draw the wings closed, and push them through the holes in the wall. If you're measured correctly in step 5), the holes will line up perfectly. As soon as they get through, they will snap open inside the hollow space. Now turn to one of the two bolts. Pull the head all the way toward you. Without using a screwdriver, begin turning the head clockwise *continuing to pull the head toward you all the while.* This will keep the toggle firm against the inside wall. Make sure you don't turn the bolt counterclockwise, or the toggle will drop off inside the wall.

9.) Turn the bolt head clockwise as far as it will go. The last few turns will have to be with a screwdriver. At this point, the toggle will begin exerting its grip on the cabinet.

10.) Repeat this process with the remaining toggle bolt. The final hold will have surprising strength.

Solid Walls

A thick concrete or brick surface is going to present more of an obstacle than a hollow one, so try

to limit the array of hangings you display on solid walls. If the time comes when you must deal with them, however, there are ways to get by. An advanced reference in home repair will discuss such hardware items as ram-set nails and expansion shields, but there we'll confine ourselves to two devices, *lead anchors* and *cut nails*—the only ones we've ever found necessary in our work.

First, remember this: in general, plastic anchors are right for plaster, lead anchors for masonry. But many solid walls are faced with lath and plaster or sheetrock, exactly like the hollow walls described in the last section. If this is the case, you can and should use *plastic anchors* for fastening things, *provided the object is light enough so that the anchor won't have to penetrate the masonry.* If you're dealing with something quite heavy, on the other hand, a large anchor will be needed, and that's when lead shields become necessary.

How to Install a Lead Anchor

To install a lead anchor, you follow exactly the same procedure as for a plastic anchor with two important differences:

Your power drill must be fitted with a carbide-tipped bit, designed to penetrate masonry. With a solid wall, you don't want to drill any more deeply than necessary because the anchor won't hold as well with air space behind it. A good trick is to mark the depth of the anchor on your bit by attaching a piece of tape to it. Once installed, the anchors are attached to your particular object with wood or lag screws.

Masonry Nails

Finally, the masonry nail, which is used when you want to hammer directly into a solid wall instead of screwing it into an anchor. It doesn't make for quite as firm a hold as a screw, but it's sufficient for hanging a great variety of decorative items, such as a copper pot or utensil rack on a brick wall. When you drive them, use a sledge, and *hammer slowly*, or you will chip the surface. In fact, you'll probably chip the surface some even if you do hammer slowly.

WALLS: PATCHING

Overview

1.) Examine walls for cracks, holes, crumbling,

peeling, bulging, or anything else that spoils the smoothness of the surface.

2.) Decide whether the wall is worth repairing or needs replacement.

3.) Gather the necessary materials.

4.) Fill in all cracks and holes.

5.) Sand down everything that has been patched or anything that is peeling or bulging.

First Considerations

Recently, friends told us that they had decided to have their bedroom repainted. "Are you tired of the color?" we asked. "No. It's just that when we painted it originally, we never prepared the walls, it looks terrible!" We have made worse blunders ourselves, but we heeded the warnings of those who knew better by carefully patching our walls in advance. Our friends knew what spackle was, but, like all of us, they wanted the room to be done overnight. Because they were so unhappy with the results, they lost interest in painting and are going to pay someone to do it this time. Unless you plan to panel your room, allow time to repair your surfaces before you paper or paint.

Materials

- Spackle
- Patching plaster
- Screwdriver
- Putty knives (1½", 3", and 6" blades)
- Pail of clear water
- Sponge
- Paper tape (for a sheetrock wall only)
- Joint compound
- 14" Trowel
- Small can or old dish that you are willing to sacrifice
- Orbital sander with assorted grades of sandpaper

Steps

You don't need a magnifying glass to find the flaws in a wall, although it's easy to come upon ones you didn't notice at first glance. We have found it helpful to go around with a pencil and circle or mark off the spots that need patching before taking putty knife in hand.

To Repair a Plaster Wall

1.) Find and mark the spots you plan to work on. Don't try to patch every minor imperfection! The average plaster wall in an old house has dozens upon dozens of hairline cracks, an inch or two in length, and literally the width of a strand of hair. You will see from the process that follows why it is impossible to deal with all of them. Start with those that have some width, holes, and longer cracks. When you have those taken care of, your remaining patience will determine how much fine detail work to do.

2.) At this point, instructions vary according to the size of the trouble spot. For small, shallow cracks and holes:

a.) Widen and deepen them a bit with the tip of a screwdriver so that the filler has sufficient space to adhere.

b.) Brush out any crumbled plaster from the cracks and holes.

c.) Wet the surfaces of the crack with clear water, using a sponge or even your plant mister, so that the wall does not soak up moisture from the spackle.

d.) Place a small supply of the spackle in a dish or can. Then take some on the tip of your 1½" putty knife, and press it into the crack, over-filling it somewhat. Next, smooth the surface by removing the excess with one swift motion of the putty knife across or down the newly filled spot.

smoothing off excess spackle with 1½" putty knife

e.) One application of spackle should be enough to fill a small crack, but if the surface has "sunk" a bit after it is dry, you will have to give it a second coat.

f.) Since you are not a professional plasterer, you will probably have to finish up with a bit of sanding; once the spackle is dry.

For larger, deeper cracks and holes:

a.) Enlarging the opening is not really necessary here. Just brush out any loose or crumbled plaster.

b.) Wet the surface of the crack with clear water, using a sponge or your plant mister.

c.) Use patching plaster rather than spackle. Spackle doesn't work well in big crevices because it will shrink and crack when it dries. Patching plaster is not premixed, so you will have to take the powder, approximate what you need, and add water to it. Proportions are provided on the bag, but the ideal working consistency allows for smooth spreading without any watery dripping. Apply it as you would the spackle.

d.) It is next to impossible to fill a large space completely the first time, so when the initial coat has hardened, moisten it again, and apply a second coat to level the surface perfectly. Since patching plaster is tougher than spackle, it will be harder to sand down, so the smoother you can make your final coat, better.

e.) If you have a hole that goes very deep, you may want to fill it first with something like newspaper rather than to build up the plaster in endless separate stages.

To Repair a Sheetrock Wall

Sheetrock won't chip or crack as easily as plaster, but it is particularly susceptible to dents. A couple we know moved into a new apartment building in an affluent suburb, and within the first month the husband had accidentally put his fist through the wall as he was making a point during an animated discussion. Yet, even if a homeowner or apartment dweller is careful, there can be problems.

If nailheads are sticking out:

a.) You must first hammer them in until they are just below the surface of the sheetrock. A slight dent is to be expected.

b.) Put some spackle in your dish or can, and with your small putty knife, cover each nailhead and dent. Make a swift downward movement of the knife to remove excess spackle and leave a smooth surface. If you can do this deftly, you should not have to sand these spots at all; if not, lightly sand after the spackle has dried, taking care not to sand off the paper coating on the surrounding sheetrock.

If tape has come loose: When a sheetrock wall is constructed, the seams between the pieces are joined with layers of joint compound and paper tape specially designed for this job. If the tape

and, consequently, the paint on top of it eventually come loose, the best thing to do is to

a.) gently peel off the loose portion, and
b.) apply a coat of joint compound to the seam as you would if you were building a new sheetrock wall.

If there are cracks in the sheetrock: Sheetrock does not commonly crack as readily as plaster does. When a wall settles, though, you can find cracks, especially around doors and windows. Prepare them exactly as you would on a plaster wall.

If there is a hole or dent in the sheetrock about the size of a baseball (you can adjust this accordingly to suit your own situation): a.) Cut five or six strips of joint tape, each about 2"-3" longer than the hole. b.) Spread some joint compound across the bottom of the hole and press in the first piece of tape. c.) Create a ladder effect with the tape by applying more joint compound along the top half of the tape you just put on and setting in a second piece that partially overlaps the first. d.) Continue to layer the tape until you have covered the hole, making sure to smooth the joint compound as you go. e.) Coat the entire patch with joint compound. f.) When it is dry, sand down any imperfections.

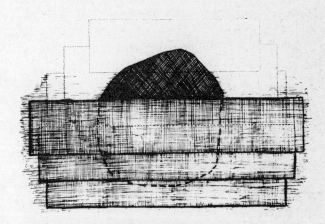

patching sheetrock wall with ladder taping technique

WALLS: REPLACEMENT

Overview

1.) Make sure that the wall must be replaced rather than patched.

2.) Measure the room to determine how much sheetrock you will need.

3.) Gather the necessary materials.

4.) Prepare the room for the job.

5.) Remove the old sheetrock or plaster, where necessary.

6.) Cut and nail in new sheetrock.

7.) Apply joint compound and tape.

8.) Sand down any imperfections in the smoothness of the wall.

Our experience has so far been limited to replacing a wall surface as opposed to demolishing or rebuilding the entire inside structure—studs and all. The kind of wall work we have done, then, is actually cosmetic. If we did not replace the wall we would not have been able to paint, paper, or tile it attractively. We were literally forced into putting up our first sheetrock wall when a well-meaning friend massacred the existing one in an attempt to remove wallpaper from it.

It seems logical to replace sheetrock with new sheetrock, but why should we tell you to use it to replace plaster? Plastering is not an entirely lost art, but it is a complex one. For a beginner to attempt it is out of the question—just think of what it takes to make one little patch solid and smooth. Yet to hire someone to build one is prohibitive; it costs more than enough to get a general handyman to put up sheetrock. And since the materials themselves are inexpensive, and the job manageable, why not make the effort?

Shopping Suggestions

Even with a material as unglamorous as sheetrock, there are decisions to be made. Do you want waterproof or regular sheetrock? Do you need ½" thickness or is ⅜" enough? How many panels of sheetrock do you need?

If you go around quickly with a tape-measure, you can take down the general measurements of the area to be done. Then, keeping in mind that you will be buying 4' x 8' sheets, calculate your needs, or bring the dimensions to your lumberyard.

If you are renovating a bathroom or kitchen, you should buy waterproof sheetrock. The ordinary kind, which is fine in other rooms, may eventually rot away from steady contact with water, and then even light pressure can cause the whole wall to cave in.

The lumberyard will also sell you sheetrock (blue) nails. As described before, blue nails come in two styles—ringed and smooth. Use the ringed variety because they give a better grip.

Materials

- Crowbar
- Hammer (a heavy one if you have it)
- Electric drill
- Panels of 4' x 8' sheetrock
- Ringed sheetrock nails
- Pencil
- Tape measure or yardstick
- Saber saw
- Joint compound
- Joint tape
- Putty knives (1½", 3", and 6")
- Trowel (14")
- Orbital sander and assorted grades of sandpaper
- Furring strips
- 10d common nails
- Ladder

Steps

Prepare the Room for the Job

If you are about to rip out a sheetrock wall, there is going to be some mess involved, but when you do the same with plaster, the area is going to look like a battle zone. Our plasterer claims that you can avoid this headache by leaving the old surface, but we found several reasons why we couldn't take the easy way out. If you are working in a small room like the bathroom, there may not be space to accommodate the extra thickness of a second wall. Also, if you are working around already existing trim (doorways, window frames, and moldings), the second layer might stick out too far into the room.

So if you can't leave the old walls up, arrange whatever furniture is in the room so that it is as far as possible from the work area. That will give you room to move around and space to put your cartons. Then cover up everything—the floor, the furniture, and yourself.

2. Remove the Sheetrock or Plaster Surface Where Necessary

Tearing down the surface of a wall seems like it would take great strength, but it really doesn't. It is a messy job rather than a complex or physically taxing one. When you have your materials assembled:

a.) Look for a weak spot in the wall, perhaps where a hole exists, or use your electric drill with a large bit to bore one.

b.) Using a combination of hammer, crowbar, and any other tool you think will help, begin to rip out pieces of the walls, surface, and drop them into your carton.

c.) If you are tearing down plaster, you do not have to touch the wood lath (horizontal strips of wood or metal mesh) behind it. You will just place your new sheetrock over it.

d.) When all the plaster or sheetrock is down, do a quick cleanup of the room.

3. Cut and Nail in New Sheetrock

The key to the successful cutting and nailing of sheetrock lies in following one simple rule: always cut the pieces so that the beginning and end of each one can be nailed to the center of a stud. If they don't, you will have nothing to nail into, and the ends won't lie perfectly flat.

Since each wall must be examined individually, no plan for piecing the sheetrock can be designed for walls in general. It is tempting to want to use as many whole panels as you can because it involves less work, but that's not usually possible. Like it or not, you will probably have to cut pieces to make them end on a stud.

a.) Take down some basic meaurements of the wall including the distance from stud to stud, so that you can decide how to place the sheets and where you will have to make cuts. Make chalk marks on the floor and/or ceiling to indicate the location of the studs.

b.) The sheets can be applied with the long side placed either horizontally or vertically; the measurements you just took will help you to decide which way to hold them. Make a plan for your wall, remembering to begin and end each piece in the center of a stud, make as few seams as possible, have as few seams as possible at eye level. The first time you can't use a full panel, measure the size of the piece you do need, and transfer those measurements to the front of the panel with a pencil and yardstick. Although you can use a utility knife to score the surface along the pencil line(s) and then snap it off, we prefer to use our saber saw (medium blade).

c.) Nail in your first piece, resting a thin length of wood between the bottom of the sheetrock and the floor to keep the panel in position slightly above the floor as you hammer the blue nails into the studs across the top. Then remove the wood strip, and continue the nailing process, hammering them in along the studs at intervals of 8"-12". Hit the nails in slightly below the surface. This will create slight dents in the sheetrock, but they will be covered over with joint compound later on.

d.) Nail in the second piece. Each piece of sheetrock should be butted to the end of the one next to it and/or on top of it.

Since sheetrock is naturally tapered along the 8' sides to allow for smooth seaming of the panels, wherever possible, butt them and make as few seams with the 4' sides as you can. Cut ends and 4' sides are best placed at the floor or ceiling.

e.) Make cutouts for electrical outlets before nailing a piece in. To do this, measure the distance of the outlet from the floor and ceiling directly on the sheetrock and mark how far into the center of the panel the opening should go. Then drill a hole in the marked off area large enough to fit the blade of your saber saw, and saw an opening just larger than the outlet itself. The rough edges will be covered by a light or switch plate later on.

f.) Finish nailing in any remaining sheetrock, and then get ready with your joint tape and joint compound.

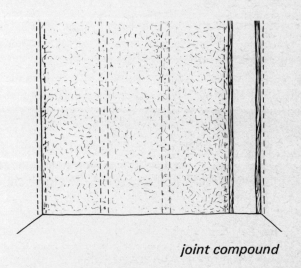

joint compound

4. Apply the Joint Tape and Joint Compound

Joint compound, which sounds like some exotic new substance, is really another name for spackle.

a.) Take a quantity of joint compound on your 6" putty knife, and fill in the space created by the seam.

b.) Cut a piece of paper tape the length of the seam, and imbed it in the tape.

c.) Now you must cover the tape with several *thin* layers of joint compound. Use your 14" trowel this time to apply the first coat, making a smooth, swift stroke along the tape. The trowel covers a wider area, which is necessary in order to blend the seam in with the rest of the wall. After the first layer has been applied, let it dry before giving it another thin coat. The key here is not to use too much joint compound at one time. Two coats may be enough to cover, but a third might prove necessary (plasterers do three).

d.) Corners are taped in much the same way as regular seams, but the tape must be folded down the center before imbedding it in the joint compound.

e.) Cover the nailheads with joint compound.

5. Sand Down Any Imperfections in the Smoothness of the Wall

As with patching, it is very rare that a professional plasterer has to use a sander on his seams, but if yours are not totally smooth, go over them lightly with the orbital sander fitted with a fine grade of paper.

CEILINGS

Since ceilings and walls are made from the same materials and function in similar ways, repairing and replacing them are nearly identical. The processes may be similar, but this time everything must be done above your head. That's not a difference you'll be likely to forget often as you work.

If you have a damaged ceiling, you have several choices. You can patch the cracks and holes, cover up the unsightliness by stuccoing the entire ceiling, or put up a new sheetrock surface.

Patching

Cracks and holes in a ceiling are filled in the same way as those in a wall; you might only use a little less water when mixing your patching plaster for the larger openings because a thicker mix will stay up more effectively.

Stuccoing

Although oppressive when overused, an occassional stucco ceiling can be considered as an element of the room's decor and, even more important, is a simple and inexpensive way to mask an ugly ceiling. If the plaster is crumbling profusely, or the sheetrock is badly sagging, then, of course, stucco is not an answer—it isn't a miracle cure. But for covering a network of cracks, it's perfect.

When we were at our local lumberyard one day, we were surprised to learn that they recommended plain old joint compound to create a stucco ceiling. There are other materials that can achieve similar effects, ranging from mortar mix to paint, but we worked with the joint compound and liked it.

To Stucco a Ceiling:

a.) Take the measurements of the ceiling so that the salesperson can help you determine how much joint compound you will need. The cheapest way to buy it is premixed in five-gallon buckets, but don't worry if you need just a bit more than one bucket. Buy the extra one. Joint compound is always good to have around, and there is a way to keep it fresh indefinitely. When you finish using it, cover it with about two inches of water before putting the lid back on. This precaution will keep it moist until you are ready to use it again; at that time, simply pour off the excess water.

b.) Gather these materials: the joint compound, a smaller bucket or container to work from, a trowel, a ladder, and drop cloths.

c.) Cover everything with dropcloths.

d.) Fill your working container with joint compound.

e.) Position the ladder at your starting corner, and climb up with your container and trowel.

f.) Scoop up a good quantity of joint compound on the working surface of the trowel (the side without the handle), and apply it by pressing the trowel to the ceiling in an up and down motion, as if you were patting it on. The up and down movement creates the stuccoed effect.

g.) Move the trowel with a free hand, swirling

it around occasionally, avoiding uniform texture. The only thing to beware of is radically changing your style or touch midway into the job. As soon as you have patted on one trowel full, go on to another and another until you have completed the job.

Replacing a Ceiling

One of our biggest failures to date concerns the ceiling we tried to put up in our guest room. Actually it was the ceiling that we *did* put up, may it rest in peace. Luck must have been with us the first time we used sheetrock in our bathroom because the first panel naturally ended on studs, and we had a secure wall without even knowing the rule that is now imbedded in our memories: Always begin and end a piece of sheetrock on a stud.

We embarked on the ceiling job blindly and fearlessly, supporting the old adage about ignorance being bliss. Within minutes we both knew the job of hoisting and balancing the bulky panels of sheetrock above our heads was too much, but instead of quitting, we were bullishly determined to get the job done. So for hours with arms raised, we stood—on ladders and desk tops—and cursed, shouted, and literally cried in pain as we pushed ahead. Then came the deadly moment of reckoning. When the sheetrock was up, we saw that there were major sags in several places. Only then did we realize that it was because we had not ended each piece on a beam; in fact, it wasn't nailed to anything. We were so devastated and ashamed at our stupidity that it took us weeks to call in a professional to redo everything. It was only from an old-time plasterer that we learned the right way to put up a sheetrock ceiling:

a.) Make a plan as you did for the walls, taking down the dimensions of the ceiling and measuring the distance between beams so that you can decide where to cut and place the sheetrock.

b.) Decide whether or not you need to remove the old ceiling. If it must come down, remove it at this point. Although we almost always found this necessary with a wall, the ceiling is one surface that can very well stay put.

Unless it is too low to begin with, leave it up. If you do, find the beams, and, to insure a firm hold for the new sheetrock, go to a lumberyard and buy some relatively thin (1" x 2") wood called furring strips, enough to cover the length of each beam in the ceiling. Nail in the furring strips along the beams, using 10d common nails.

c.) Before lifting the sheetrock anywhere, construct two "T"-shaped structures, each nailed together with two furring strips as indicated, with the top piece lying flat.

1"x 2" furring strip
measuring 1' long

1"x 2" furring strip
measuring ½" longer than
the distance from floor
to ceiling

Later, when these Ts are wedged in tightly (the 1" x 2" strips have enough "give" to do this well), they will hold the sheetrock, leaving you free for nailing.

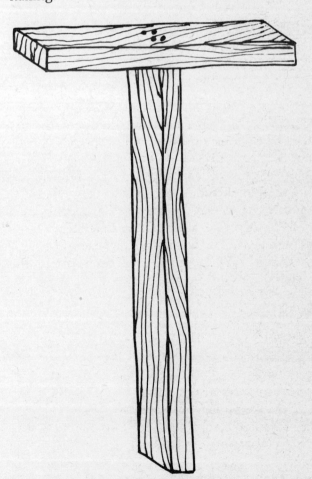

the "T" brace for installing sheetrock

d.) Place a ladder in the middle of the area where you will be putting up the first piece; rest your Ts against it so that they are within easy reach.

e.) Take your first piece of sheetrock (the principles and instructions for placing and cutting are the same as for a wall), and raise it above you, placing the center of the panel on your head.

f.) Carefully approach the ladder, and climb up two or three steps, depending on your height, so that you are standing as high as you can go.

g.) Grab a T and wedge it in, in front of you; use the other T to do the same behind you. Once they are up, adjust their positions so that the Ts are at either end of the sheetrock.

h.) Nail in the first piece (into the furring strips, if you have put them up) as you would any sheetrock, and remove the Ts. Repeat the entire procedure for the rest of the ceiling.

i.) Apply joint compound and tape to the seams, and cover the nailheads.

WINDOWS

First Considerations

When the windows are not giving us any trouble, we really don't give them much thought. But just try to open a window that's stuck, perhaps breaking the glass in the process, or struggle to keep a window open when its sash cord is broken, and suddenly the window becomes a major headache. Since most of our dealings with windows have been limited to their repair and maintenance (as opposed to installation or replacement), we'll cover the four most common problems in this chapter.

Materials

For Unsticking a Window
- Block of wood
- Hammer
- Putty knife or thin chisel
- Electric sander with sandpaper
- Touch-up paint
- Machine oil

For Replacing Screen
- Screening
- Screwdriver
- Scissors
- Staplegun with staples
- Brads
- Utility knife

For Replacing Glass
- Glass cut to size
- Work gloves
- Pliers
- Glazing compound (putty)
- Putty knife
- Glazier's points
- Screwdriver

For Replacing Broken Sash Cords
- Sash chain and Hardware
- Hammer
- 3″ Putty knife
- Old Screwdriver
- Nail
- Pliers
- Toothpick (if necessary)
- Hacksaw (or wire cutting pliers)

Basic Windows

In addition to the basic windows that all houses have, there is also probably a full set of storm windows. But within these two categories are several varieties. The most common kind of basic window, especially in older or traditionally designed newer homes, is the double-hung window. It has a wood frame which comes in two parts that can move up and down. Each part is called a sash, and what enables the sashes to move into a given position and stay there is a system of weighted cord or chain that runs through a set of pullies. All this magic is neatly hidden within the wood molding that surrounds the window unit. Sometimes the sash is also made up of several smaller pieces of glass, each surrounded by its own strips of wood called mullions.

If a house does not have double-hung windows, it probably has casement windows, the kind with metal frames that open outward. These operate on hinges, and you open and close them with a latch or a rotating handle.

There are other kinds, like sliding or stationary windows, but they are not very common.

Different storm windows are made to fit the various windows just described, and they usually

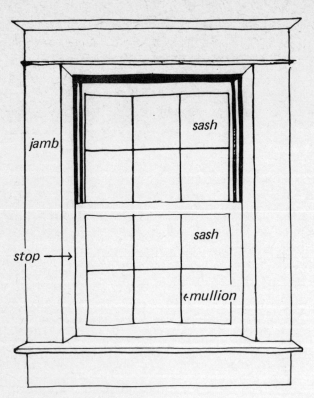

the double hung window

go hand in hand with similarly designed screens.

Years ago the only kind of storm window or screen you could have for a double-hung window was what is called the self-hung type. The storms and screens are separate, built into their own wooden frames, and at the beginning and end of a season, the homeowner must hook the one he wants onto the outside of the regular window. They look fine and basically do their job, but they have several drawbacks. Not only are the storms heavy and thus potentially dangerous to install on upper floors, but the seasonal switching takes hours and never seems to get done in time for the unexpected heat wave or cold snap.

Permanently installed combination storms and screens eliminate these problems. The frames are made of aluminum and the permanently baked-on colors never need repainting. They are called "combination" because the storm window and the screen are set into one frame, and you have only to slide them up and down to get the one you want. In minutes you can winterize the whole house. It is possible to buy the combination windows and install them yourself, but we strongly advise against this. The real expense is for the

window, not the installation. Also, unless your windows are perfect rectangles, and surprisingly few are, you have to adjust them to the slope of the opening. This takes time and skill to do if you want the fit to be as airtight as possible. In some states, if the company does the work, you also pay no sales tax because the installation job is considered a home improvement.

If you have casement windows, the storms and screens are separate, and, surprisingly, they are placed inside the regular casement window. You install them or remove them by turning a series of latches that keep the storm or screen in place.

WINDOWS: PROBLEMS YOU MAY ENCOUNTER

Unsticking a Window

We have found that there is not one simple solution that solves the problem every time, but before you pick up any tools, see if you can locate the part of the window that's stuck. It may be the whole thing, but often a side can rattle back and forth, leaving only one side that is causing the trouble.

For a Double-hung Window:

1.) Check to see if the window is even slightly open—it can be stuck in an open position. If you are dealing with the bottom sash, place a block of wood on top of it, and strike it in a downward direction with a hammer. The blows on the wood may break the seal that is making the window stick. For the top sash, hold the wood block at its base, and strike it in an upward direction.

2.) Hold a putty knife or thin chisel to a spot that seems to be stuck, placing it between the wood of the sash and the surrounding trim. Then take a hammer, and gently tap the putty tool into the crack to loosen the window.

3.) As a last measure, take the whole window out by prying off the side moldings (called the stops) that hold it in place and disengaging the sash cord. This is a rather drastic step, but if you choose to do this, while the window is out, take your electric sander, and smooth down the heavily painted side surfaces of each sash. Then reconnect the sash cords, and secure the window by replacing the stops.

After you have opened a stuck window, you will want to learn how to prevent it from happening again. Unfortunately, there are no guarantees. Often it is the weather and not paint that is the problem. The only things you can keep in mind are:

1.) Never shut a newly painted window all the way until it is dry; even a small opening can help you later on. In fact, if you can move the window up and down a few times as it dries, that can keep it from sticking altogether.

2.) Don't apply a new coat of paint to a sash that is already heavily laden with old paint until you have sanded the areas that could possibly stick.

For a Casement Window:

If a casement window is stuck because of paint that has dried, you treat it as you would a double-hung one: try to break the seal that has been created, using your putty knife and hammer.

If paint is not the problem, then perhaps the window's hinges and latches need oiling. Apply machine oil, and after it has had a chance to be absorbed, try to open the window.

As with double-hung windows, you can prevent sticking in the future by sanding down heavily painted or rusty areas and then taking care when painting not to let the window dry in any one position, especially closed. If you also oil its moving parts regularly, the problems should be eliminated.

Replacing Glass and Screen

To Replace Screen in a Self-hung Wood Frame:

1.) Measure the opening to be screened and add ½" on each side for the needed overlap. Go to your local hardware store, and buy replacement screening.

2.) Gently pry off the thin wooden molding on the side that covers the edges of the screen.

3.) Remove the old screen by lifting out staples with a screwdriver.

4.) If the screen you have bought is larger than what you need, trim it to size. Be very careful to mark the screen, adding that extra half inch all around before you cut.

5.) Fold the screen over ½" down one long side.

6.) Take a staple gun and staple the screen at the top and bottom along that edge, stretching the screen as tautly as possible, followed by one in the middle. Then go back, and put a staple about every inch between those already in.

7.) Follow the same procedure on the other long side and then on the shorter sides.

8.) When the screen is in place, put the molding back on. If the old nails are no longer usable, replace them with new ones (brads).

To Replace Screen in a Combination Window:

1.) Snap the screen out of the window frame.

2.) If you turn the screen over so that the outside faces you, you will notice a border of thin rubber tubing set into a space between the screen and its frame. This tubing is what keeps the screen in place, and it can easily be removed and replaced when you want to put in new screens.

3.) After you have removed the tubing and pulled off the old screen, measure the new screen to fit the opening and include an extra ½" overlap on each side.

4.) Stretch the screen over the frame, and then begin to fit the rubber tubing into its space, pulling the screen as tautly as possible. A screwdriver can help you wedge the tube in if you have any trouble. If the overlapping screen sticks out, cut it off with a utility knife.

Glass windows are not quite as easy to replace as screens since they're breakable and potentially dangerous. Therefore, proceed with caution.

To Replace Glass in a Window with a Wood Frame:

1.) Go to the hardware or glass store with the exact measurements of the space to be filled. If you tell the salesperson that your figures represent the total opening, he will adjust them properly for you, making them slightly smaller.

2.) Put on a pair of gloves to protect your hands as you remove the old glass, putty, and small metal triangles called glazier's points from the window. A pair of pliers may help.

3.) Place a thin ribbon of glazing compound in the channel where the glass will go.

4.) Put the glass in place in its triangle.

5.) Replace the glazier's points—either the ones you took out or, if they are bent out of shape, new ones. You can't use a hammer to tap them in because they must be flush to the glass to keep it in place. Instead, push each one in, pointy tip first, with the flat side of a screwdriver.

6.) When the glass is in place, use glazing compound on the outside to seal it. Take your putty knife, and apply a band of the compound all around between the wood and the glass, and smooth it at an angle so that it is tapered, getting thicker as you go onto the wood (use another window for reference).

7.) Put the sash temporarily in place. Take a tape measure, place it against the side of the pulley where the weight will sit, and bend it around and down the sash to the small hole below the groove mentioned in step 3). Mark this distance on the chain, BUT ADD AN INCH OR TWO. You can always remove more later if you have to.

8.) Cut the correct length of chain with your hacksaw or wire-cutting pliers.

9.) Tap a small nail halfway into the jamb just below the pulley. Attach one end of the chain temporarily so that the chain doesn't slip off while you secure the other end to the weight.

10.) Thread the chain over the pulley, push the lower end through the hole at the top of the weight, and attach it permanently with the triangular piece of hardware.

11.) Replace the weight inside the pocket. The chain is now attached to the top of the weight, and you're going to finish the job by attaching the other end to the slot in the top side of the sash.

12.) Remove the free end of the chain from the nail, and slip it through the groove so that it comes out the hole.

13.) Take the spiral-shaped piece of hardware and wedge the last link of the chain under the coiled metal with a pliers. Then bend it down tightly to fasten. Remove the nail from the jamb.

14.) Put the sash back in place. The downward force of the weight should pull the coiled metal up snug against the hole.

15.) Raise the window up all the way. If the weight falls too far and hits the sill, you really have no choice but to take everything out again and cut away a few links of chain. This is painful, but it's better than cutting the chain too short.

16.) Replace the wooden wedge, and screw it in place again. Use some bits of toothpick to narrow the hole if necessary.

17.) If both cords are being replaced, repeat the procedure for the other side.

18.) Replace the stops; sand and repaint if you

have done any damage to the woodwork.

The preceeding directions apply primarily to wooden double-hung windows and self-hung storms. The same procedure can be adapted to casement windows. Most aluminum storms these days, however, do not use the putty method when replacing the glass. These windows are "marine glazed" in the factory and secured by rubber stripping and screws. We have never replaced the glass in these so we hesitate to give you advice. What we will probably do when the time comes is snap out the window and bring it to a glass store (cheaper than calling them in) and let them repair it.

Replacing a Broken Sash Cord

Earlier, we described the cord and pulley system that enables double-hung windows to open and close. In most older homes, you'll find plain old clothesline rope used for sash cords. Since the windows can't function unless these cords are operating properly, you may as well make replacing broken ones a top priority.

To Replace Sash Cord:

1.) Remove all obstructions (curtains, rods, window shades, etc.).

2.) Pry off the stops by tapping a 3" putty knife with a hammer into the cracks that separate them from the rest of the trim molding. At first, it may be hard to see this separation because coats of paint often obscure it, but probe gently and you'll strike it.

3.) When the sash is free, tilt it out toward you. Assuming that both cords don't need to be replaced, the remaining one should be sufficient to support the window while you work. At the top of each side of the sash you'll notice a groove with a small hole under it. This is where the broken cord should be attached. Unknot and remove it.

4.) Now examine the window jamb. Towards the bottom, look closely and you'll see a detachable piece of wood held in with a single screw. It may take a few moments to find this under the generations of paint that have obscured it. When you locate the screw, tap away the accumulated paint with a hammer and old screwdriver, and take it out. The wood is wedged shaped at the bottom, so be careful about how you try to remove it. You'll probably have to attack it from all sides:

loosening paint from the grooves, tapping away with your hammer, prying the blade of the putty knife below the lower edge of the block of wood.

5.) Once the wood is out, you'll be able to see the weight sitting inside the pocket behind the jamb. Take it out, and untie and discard the other half of the broken sash cord.

6.) What you're going to do now is to replace the old cord with chain, secure it to the weight, thread it over the pulley, and attach it to the top of the sash. The first step is to measure and cut the chain. If you think ahead for a moment, you'll be able to understand just how long it needs to be before you do the actual cutting. When the window is fully closed, the weight should sit just below the pulley; when the window is fully open, it should sit just *above* the sill, but not *on* it (you still want it to exert its downward pull).

Chapter 6

Wallpaper

Overview

1.) Measure the surfaces being prepared.
2.) Shop for, select, and order the wallpaper.
3.) Gather the necessary materials.
4. Remove any old paper from the walls, where necessary.
5.) Prepare the walls for papering.
6.) Organize the room for the job.
7.) Apply the paper.

First Considerations

Although wallpapering is a popular do-it-yourself task, you might want to begin modestly to see if wallpapering is your forte. We chose a relatively inexpensive and easy-to-hang paper and applied it to one of our bedroom walls. We were reluctant to begin our paperhanging with the costly, custom-colored paper we used later on.

The best reason for bypassing the professional is usually the money you save. But today there is an even more compelling reason: the master craftsman is rarely to be found anymore, and those who do try to bill themselves as skilled artisans, charging fancy prices, often do work of embarrassingly poor quality. In recent months, we have seen a foyer in which the print was obviously mismatched, a kitchen where edges of wallpaper hung loose, a bathroom where the wrong glue had been applied to foil paper and had begun to show through.

To do a wallpapering job yourself, you need a solid block of time when you are relatively free from interruptions, the necessary materials, a partner to work with (if possible), and this set of simple instructions.

As you get ready to visit the wallcovering stores, make sure to measure your walls. If any of them is broken up by windows, doors, or permanent obstructions, a diagram with accurate dimensions will help the dealer calculate your needs.

Shopping Suggestions

Overchoice is always a problem when shopping, but the word takes on new meaning when applied to wallpaper. The feeling is something akin to drowning, but instead of water, the medium is paper, vinyl, foil, flocking, or fabric. A well-stocked store will have hundreds of books, each with dozens of designs in assorted colors. The styles range from daringly modern to cautiously conservative, and the price per roll also varies drastically, from a few dollars to over one hundred. Even with trained sales help working with you, you are likely to become something of a fixture at the store until you've made your choice. Occasionally you know instantly what you want, or something you already own dictates the color or design. Then your job is easy. But overchoice is bound to get you sooner or later—if not in the kitchen, then in the bedroom.

Sometimes you know the kind of pattern you want and have seen dozens that are *almost* right but find something holding you back each time. What you may really need is a paper custom colored to your specifications. This does not mean that you must design the print yourself; rather, you find a pattern offered by a company that does customized work and substitute your own colors for the ones shown in the book. Naturally you can expect to pay for such a privilege, mainly because these papers are often the costly ones to begin with, but, from time to time, you may just want to splurge. For the coloring itself, expect to be charged a flat fee in addition to the price of the paper, but this price is usually a relatively small part of the total bill.

As if problems of choice were not enough, add to it the difficulty of visualizing an entire room in a pattern based on the small sample in the book. To help you choose appropriately, ask yourself these questions:

Is the room very small? If so, a large bold print might be inadvisable.

Is the room in a dark or light part of the house? A dark room could profit from a cheery paper.

Is the room used often? A sturdy, water-resistant, easy-to-clean paper might be more suitable here than a delicate one.

Is this your first wallpapering job? If it is, you may want suggestions for a simple design and an inexpensive paper.

Before you place your order, make sure that you are aware of the store's return policy. If you order a stock paper from a reputable store, you should be able to return any unused full rolls and get your money back minus a service charge. Custom papers, understandably, are never returnable. With these orders, the store may send someone to your house to measure, at no extra charge, to avoid problems when there are no returns. Otherwise, bringing the measurements to the store is the only answer.

Materials

For Removing Old Wallpaper
- Commercially sold wallpaper remover (or steamer, where necessary)
- Pail
- Large brush
- Scraper
- Steel wool
- Cartons or large plastic trash bags

For preparing the Wall
- Spackle
- Putty knife
- Electric sander
- Assorted grades of sandpaper
- Sizing (primer-sealer)
- Large brush
- Scraper

For Applying the Paper
- Wallpaper
- Yardstick
- Pencil
- Scissors
- Razor knife
- Wide wall scraper
- Large sponge
- Seam roller
- Plumb line (string cut to be as long as the height of a typical wall, a weight, a tack, and colored chalk)
- Working surface
- Ladder
- Waterbox or watertray (for pre-pasted paper only)
- Recommended adhesive for your paper
- Paint roller with extension pole
- Roller tray

Steps

It is such a natural impulse to want to start this job by gluing your first piece of paper right to the wall. No one wants days to go by with the room looking progressively *worse* after hours of toil. Now is the time, then, to brace yourself for the rather long preparatory period that precedes the day you can begin filling the room with color.

1. Remove Any Old Wallpaper from Walls, Where Necessary

If you are planning to paper a painted wall or a new wall, go directly to the next step. You can put your wallcovering over already existing paper under certain circumstances: if the wall below is quite smooth, if the old paper is still firmly glued to the wall in most places, if there are not many old layers underneath it, and if the texture of the old paper will allow for a firm bond with the new paper (consult your dealer). Those are a lot of ifs, but even with all these qualifications met, it is always better to start clean, especially if the wall is plaster.

The kind of walls you have, plaster or sheetrock, and the type of wallcovering to be removed will determine the method of paper removal you follow.

For Plaster Walls
If the paper is of the "strippable" variety,

a.) simply start at the bottom in a corner where an edge is exposed, and give the paper a tug. It should start to come away from the wall in complete strips if you pull evenly and gently.

b.) Keep a carton or plastic trash bag handy to put the paper into as you go along.

c.) If you have removed a vinyl paper, its paper backing may remain on the wall. It is fine, even recommended, to leave this on as long as it adheres firmly. If it is not on firmly, or if the manufacturer of your new paper says to remove it, you must do so as you would with regular paper.

If the paper is not strippable,

a.) Ask your dealer to recommend one of the concentrated products which will soak the paper off the wall.

b.) Follow the directions on the product you have bought, keeping in mind that there are going to be stubborn spots which won't come off immediately. You may have to apply the liquid many times to such spots and work with your scraper. Protect the floors, too, because these wet, sticky pieces of paper can really get messy. Spread newspaper down before you begin, and if you must leave the work area, take off your shoes. Keep plenty of empty cartons handy, too.

The old-fashioned way to remove wallpaper was with a steamer. While these cumbersome machines are available for rental, they are rarely used today except when you have to remove paper from sheetrock. This is a thankless job which you should do only if it is absolutely impossible to leave the old paper up.

For Sheetrock Walls

When we moved into our house, we couldn't wait to remove the hideous wallpaper we found in our upstairs bathroom. So when a friend volunteered to help us out one day, we eagerly set him up with a bucket of soaking preparation. We were sadly unaware that he was starting one of only three sheetrock walls in the entire house. Only after our friend mutilated the wall, removing layers of the sheetrock along with the wallpaper, did we learn that there had to be another way.

You will avoid many hours of hard labor if you can leave the old paper up. To ready it for the new paper, just sand down the seams and any imperfections, glue down any loose spots, and

then apply a priming substance specially designed to help paper stick to an already papered wall.

2. Prepare the Walls for Papering

In order for a wall to be prepared, it must be smooth, clean, and sized (more about that word later). Although the condition of an unpapered wall is obvious from the beginning, all sorts of little surprises may await you underneath that old layer of paper—cracks, bulges, holes, and old paint. Even a relatively good surface will need some care, especially if paper has just been removed from it.

To Prepare a Plaster Wall

a.) If you have just removed wallpaper, you must make sure that small bits of paper or paste do not remain on the bare surface. Some water and fine steel wool will remove these traces.

b.) If the wall had previously been painted, make sure none of it is peeling off. If it is, scrape the area with a scraper, and then sand it down to remove any gloss from the surface that would prevent the paper from sticking properly.

c.) Repair all cracks.

d.) After they have thoroughly dried, sand down all newly patched areas (first with a coarse and then a finer grade of sandpaper) as well as any places where the old plaster is either rough or bulging.

e.) Wash the walls down with some ammonia and water followed by a clear water rinse to remove any dirt, dust, soap, or grease.

f.) Remove any electrical outlet or switch plates from the walls.

g.) Clean the floors and surfaces of all dirt and dust.

h.) Apply sizing or a primer-sealer. These serve basically the same function: to act as a base which seals the old surface so the wallpaper will slide smoothly onto the wall, and to prevent anything on the wall (paint, spackle) from causing trouble. Follow the directions on the container of the product you choose, allowing sufficient drying time before you paper. Just be aware that sealers for wallpaper are not the same as those for paint.

To Prepare a Sheetrock Wall

If you must prepare a sheetrock wall, follow the same procedure as you would with a plaster wall, with these precautions:

a.) Use a very light touch when sanding because the top layers of sheetrock are paper.

b.) When washing down or priming the wall, allow at least a day for it to dry because this kind of wall absorbs liquid readily.

c.) Check for exposed nails, and if you find any, hammer them in, spackle each spot in stages, and sand when the spackle is dry.

d.) If you have decided to leave the old wallpaper up, make sure to use a primer over it that is made especially to help bond paper to paper.

3. Organize the Room for the Job

Remove as much as you can from the room and cover anything valuable with drop cloths. The only thing you would specifically want to retain is a desk or large table to use as a cutting surface. If you don't have anything like that, you can set one up in an adjoining room.

4. Apply the Paper

Although wallpaper does rip and should not be mistreated purposely, it is not nearly as fragile as you might think. So proceed slowly, try not to panic if something goes wrong, and keep your sense of humor as you follow these directions (along with any special instructions that come with the paper).

a.) Bring in all the materials.

b.) Mark the plumb line. A plumb line is used to indicate a true vertical on the wall. Quite often the walls are not exactly perpendicular to the floors and ceilings. The wallpaper, however, must be.

To mark a plumb line, go to the least noticed corner of the room and measure out to a point that is ½'' *less* than the width of your wallpaper (e.g., if your paper is 27'' wide, measure to a point that is 26½'' from the corner). Do this at three different heights between the ceiling and the floor. Since the three marks may not fall directly below one another, look for the one that is closest to the corner.

Apply chalk to the plumb line cord, and tack it at the ceiling so that it falls and hits the point you just located. When the plumb line has stopped moving, pull it taut. While holding it taut, snap the string so it hits the wall, leaving a colored line from the chalk.

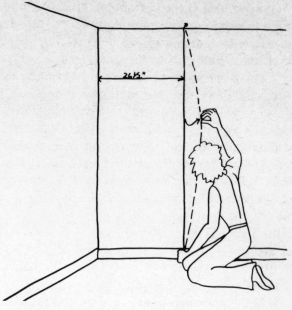

marking plumb line

Remove the plumb line and tack.

c.) To cut the first piece of wallpaper, take the whole roll of paper to the wall, and measure out a piece that is at least 4'' longer than you need to go from the top of the wall to the baseboard. Mark the roll with a pencil at the right spot. Bring the roll to your cutting surface, and cut across at the spot you had marked, being sure to do it evenly along a straight line. CUT ONLY ONE PIECE AT A TIME.

Some sources advise you to cut several pieces of wallpaper at a time, matching them up on the table rather than on the wall. We think this is a mistake. If you cut as you go, you can account for the unexpected, and if you have made a mistake it is just with one piece. If you have cut six pieces, all may be ruined.

d.) Hang the first piece. This step depends upon the paper you are using.

For paper requiring paste, apply the adhesive directly to the *wall* with a roller. It is infinitely easier to position a dry piece of paper than one covered with paste; we have done it both ways.

a.) Pour a quantity of adhesive into a paint roller making sure that it isn't too thick to handle. If you are using a premixed adhesive, the directions may warn you not to add water, but we did so anyway after finding it impossible to maneuver the paper on the wall. Later, our wallpaper dealer suggested that we always dilute the adhesive, using approximately one-half quart of water to a gallon of paste.

b.) Get a pail of lukewarm clear water.

c.) Take a paint roller to which you have attached an extension pole, and roll it into the paste.

d.) Bring the roller to your starting spot.

e.) Roll the paste evenly onto the wall, unroll the strip of wallpaper, and line one side up along the plumb line with the other lapping into the corner and onto the next wall. The top and bottom edges should each overlap the ceiling and baseboard, respectively, by about 2'' giving you extra paper that will soon be trimmed off.

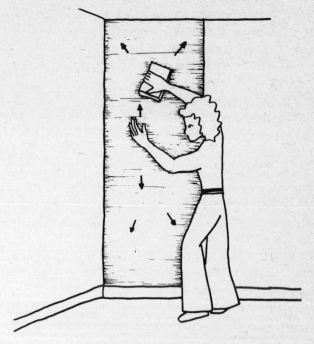

smoothing out paper with a sponge

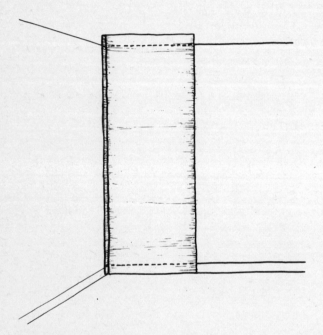

putting up first piece

wall slightly at the top, fold along the crease, and cut with the scissors along the fold with as steady a hand as possible. Then smooth the top edge back up.

h.) Repeat the same process at the bottom to trim excess paper at baseboards.

f.) Immediately take a clean, wet sponge, and start smoothing out the paper that is likely to be far from smooth now and full of air bubbles underneath. Press down quite hard as you smooth out the top in an upward direction, followed by downward strokes to secure the bottom. Then brush the sponge to the sides until the entire strip is smooth. Be sure that both sides are firm to the wall, applying more adhesive to the edges, with your finger, if necessary.

g.) With a wide wall scraper and scissors, trim the top and bottom edges. Use the scraper to push the paper to the ceiling and make a crease that follows the ceiling line (or the molding line if the trim is already up). Pull the paper away from the

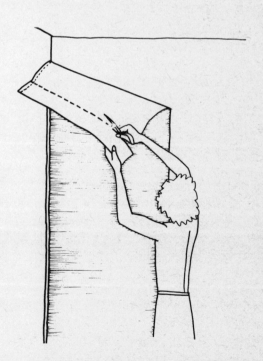

trimming paper with scissors

i.) When the strip is in place again and totally smooth, wash it down with a clean sponge to remove any excess adhesive.

For pre-pasted paper, here are general instructions.

a.) Fill your water tray with water, usually cool-lukewarm, and place it as closely as possible to your starting point.

b.) Take the strip of paper you have just cut, and roll it loosely, starting at the bottom with the pasted side *out*.

c.) Place the roll directly into the water, following the directions that came with the paper for the length of time it should be submerged.

d.) When you have removed the roll, bring it to your starting point, and unroll it as you apply it to the wall.

e.) The directions for placing, smoothing, trimming, and cleaning it are the same as for paper that is not pre-pasted.

Hang the second piece. If your paper is a vertical stripe, grasscloth, suede, or something else that requires no matching:

a.) Cut a piece 4″ longer than the measurement you need, and after you have rolled adhesive onto the wall (or submerged the pre-pasted strip in the water tray) just make sure you "butt" the side edge of the new piece to the edge of the first one. Butting means bringing the edges together so they meet tightly *without* overlapping.

b.) Smooth out the new piece in the same way as you did the first.

If you are using *a patterned paper*, before cutting the second strip,

a.) you must match the design from the roll to the piece already on the wall. That may mean wasting several feet of paper. Nothing advertises the work of an amateur more readily than mismatched paper.

In your eagerness to match a pattern, don't be folled by a section that only partially matches up. In a floral, for example, two pieces of a leaf may correspond, but if you look further down, you'll see that the petals don't. That means you must search further for the match.

b.) When you have aligned the papers, remember to allow for the extra 2″ at the top and bottom before you cut the strip.

c.) Then hang it the same way as for a nonpatterned piece, just being careful as you smooth it

out not to spoil the alignment of the pattern.

d.) Continue the same process for each remaining piece until you come to a special situation.

Special Situations. It would be nice if every piece could require a full sheet hung vertically with no obstructions or corners to get in the way. Before long, though, you are bound to come to an electrical outlet, a light switch, a door, a window, or a corner. Thus for,

a.) *Electrical outlet or light switch:* Unscrew and remove the plate covering it, if you have not done so already, and then measure and start to hang the strip as usual. When you smooth out the paper in that area, though, take a razor and cut away the paper around the switch or outlet. Any imperfections in the cutting will be covered when you replace the plate.

papering over electrical outlet

b.) *Window or door:* For the pieces that go along the length of a window or door, measure and cut as you would for an unbroken wall. Then, as with an electrical outlet, roll paper over the door or window. When it is in place on the wall sections, cut away the parts hanging over the door or window and trim edges with scissors or razor. For wall areas above or below that can take the full width of the roll, match the pattern and cut the small pieces to fit those places (there is no need here to cover the door or window).

c.) *Inside corner:* Our wallpaper dealer advised us, contrary to the more complicated traditional rules, to simply wrap the strip from one wall into

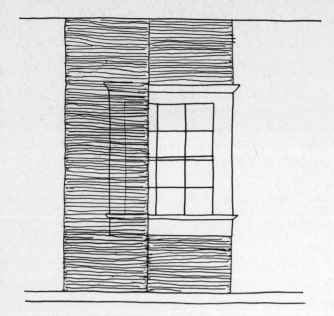

wallpapering around window

the corner onto the next wall. To do this successfully, however, you must make sure that there is plenty of adhesive in the corner, that you push the paper all the way into the corner, and that you secure its position by running down the corner gently, but firmly, with a wide scraper. Finally, smooth out the rest of the paper on the new wall.

d.) *Outside corner:* Outside corners are usually a bit easier than inside ones. If you are papering both walls involved, simply wrap the strip around the wall and proceed as usual. If your papering stops at an outside corner, you will have to cut an even line, lengthwise, a bit short of the edge so that it doesn't stick out and get torn as people brush by.

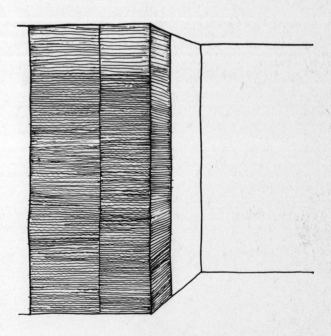

wallpapering outside corner

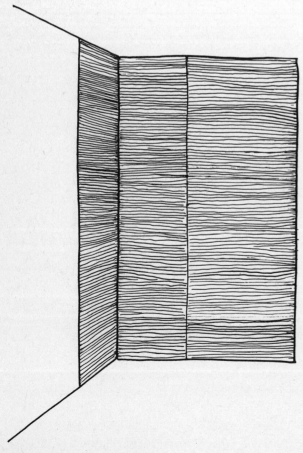

wallpapering inside corner

e.) *Ceiling:* Although a papered ceiling can be a smart decorator's touch, it is not easy to do. In fact, when cartoonists picture a do-it-yourselfer drowning in a mass of falling wallpaper, the fellow is usually trying to paper a ceiling. If you decide to attempt it observe the following:
• Make sure to do the ceiling *before* the walls.
• Prepare the ceiling just as you would any wall (spackle, sand, prime).
• Run the strips the short way, across the ceiling, so that you have less paper to handle at one time.
• Try to work with another person, one to do

the maneuvering and smoothing and the other to hold the paper up.

• Start at the end of the room that is most visible.

• Make a plumb line as you would for the walls, measuring a distance from your starting point that is ½" less than the width of your paper, but this time make your set of markings at each side. Then tack the chalked string (minus the weight) at both ends, and snap it from the center to make your line.

• Procedures for spreading the adhesive, where applicable, matching the prints and allowing for obstructions (e.g. ceiling fixture), are the same as for a regular wall—you will just be working above your head!

• When you put up the first piece, allow it to overlap onto the wall.

• When you trim your excess from the first and last strips and the ends of each strip, allow about ¼" to overlap permanently onto the walls all around if you are going to paper each adjoining wall.

• You may be surprised to learn that when you come to papering the walls, usually you can only match one wall to the ceiling. Choose the one that you think is most visible.

• If the room has ceiling molding or if you think you might like to add some, remember that it has the added advantage of covering up imperfections in the meeting of walls and ceiling.

f.) *Unusual wall protrusions:* Sometimes part of a wall, such as one that masks a pipe, is not straight. Since the possibilities for irregular shapes are endless, we can't give you any real instructions here. You just have to play it by ear, very often adding a separate piece of wallpaper to cover the protrusion. At such times, a bit of artistic ability is more valuable than mechanical skill.

Finishing Touches. It is wise to check over each wall as you finish it rather than wait until the end when everything is dry. Even though you have cleaned each strip as it has gone up, some adhesive is bound to be left. You may also find small spots where a corner or a seam has not set firmly. Dip your finger into the adhesive, where applicable, and go over the area where the curling has taken place. Then you can run down the seam or corner with your seam roller to secure it.

Chapter 7

Interior Painting

Overview

1.) Measure the area to be painted.
2.) Select and purchase the paint.
3.) Gather the necessary materials.
4.) Remove any old wallpaper, where necessary.
5.) Prepare the surfaces for painting.
6.) Organize the room for the job.
7.) Paint the surfaces.

First Considerations

Painting the interior of your own house is an ideal way to gain quick confidence as a home craftsman. For once the old line, "Even a child can do it," applies literally. There are important preparatory steps to take, and corners and ceiling lines require a deft hand, but in general the job is every bit as easy as you'd imagine it to be. You buy the paint, dip in your brush or roller, and cover the wall with color.

Here, as with our observations on wallpapering, the hired professional's record is consistently dismal. We have witnessed ceilings where large sections were obviously missed, colors that were not what the customer had chosen, surfaces that had not been appropriately prepared for painting, and often a reluctance by the painter to remedy his own mistakes.

Shopping Suggestions

Even though there is not nearly the variety of choice in paint that you will find in wallpaper, paint stores do display rack after rack of color samples—there are so many shadings of what we used to call just white or yellow or gray.

Begin your shopping knowing, generally, the color you want, the dimensions of the area to be painted, and what kind of surface you will be coating.

Your choice of color will be determined, in part, by two other factors: whether or not you are set on using a water-based or an oil-based paint and whether you want to have paint custom mixed or simply stick to the premixed varieties.

Water-based or latex paint has become the more popular choice for both interior and exterior work. Brushes and rollers can be cleaned of latex paint with plain water; spills can be wiped up easily; surfaces dry rapidly without leaving brush or roller marks; the mixture does not smell as much as oil-based paint; it can be touched up effectively; and it is washable.

Oil-based paint, however, still has its strong proponents. It is particularly good on wood, both inside and out, whereas latex paint has a tendency to peel. Also when you're choosing a very deep color, an oil base can absorb the pigment more effectively. In the ready-mixed field, in fact, we found that certain dark colors only came as exterior oil-based paint. We wanted to paint the trim around the natural wood walls in our kitchen a deep brick red, and oil base was the only kind we could find.

Premixed paints, as the name implies, are the ones that you can take off the shelf, and with all the many brands and colors, it is likely that you can find one to suit your requirements. Just be careful not to buy poor quality bargain labels in an effort to save money. Stick to name brands, or use the "house" brand if you are dealing with a reputable store.

From time to time, you may want a special

shade, perhaps to match a fabric or create an un- usual effect. Then you may be willing to spend the extra dollars for custom-mixed paint. You select the color you want from a set of paint chips, and the store blends the mixture to your order.

After you have decided between latex or oil and custom or premixed, the other decision you must make concerns "finish." Do you want the surface to look dull, shiny, or somewhat in between? The common terms for the finish a paint offers, going from dullest to glossiest, include: flat, eggshell, satin, semi-gloss, and high gloss. Terminology can differ from manufacturer to manufacturer, but a salesperson should be able to give you a sim- ple translation. The finish, like the color itself, is really a matter of taste.

Materials

For Removing Old Wallpaper
- Wallpaper remover (or steamer where necessary)
- Pail
- Large brush
- Scraper
- Steel wool
- Cartons or large plastic trash bags

For Preparing the Walls and Trim
- Spackle
- Putty knife
- Electric sander
- Assorted grades of sandpaper
- Sizing or primer-sealer
- Large brush
- Scraper
- Wood filler
- Surface preparation liquid for wood trim

For Applying the Paint
- Paints
- Roller
- Roller extension
- Assorted brushes (medium-sized, small, and extra-fine)
- Ladder
- Roller tray
- Sponge
- Bucket of clear water (for water-based paint)
- Mineral spirits (for oil-based paint)
- Rags
- Drop cloths
- Paint stirrer
- Window scraper with supply of razor blades

Steps

1. Remove Old Wallpaper from Walls, Where Necessary

Some books tell you how to save yourself time and work by painting over wallpaper. But the day will come when the wallpaper beneath will make its ugly presence known, and then you will have to deal with the problem all over again. The seams may eventually show through the paint; the paper—especially if it is boldly colored—may not be covered easily; and if the time comes when you do want to strip the wall, paint over paper will make the whole job much more difficult. Better, then, to get rid of the stuff from the beginning.

If you must keep the paper up, however, because you are afraid of removing it from un- sized sheetrock, make sure to sand down the seams, and use an oil-based paint.

2. Prepare the Surfaces for Painting

Preparing the walls for new paint is essentially the same as for wallpaper. The one difference is that you have to be even more exacting for paint preparation since the naked wall will be in full view when you have finished, and any imperfec- tions will show right through no matter how many coats of paint you apply. This is an un- glamorous job. It requires lots of patience and, quite frankly, progresses slowly, but please don't cut corners here.

Another difference is in the final preparatory step: priming. Paint primer is not the same as wallpaper primer, so check with your dealer for the product that is right for you. When painting, even when the wall is not new or previously un- painted, you may still want to prime it if you have done a lot of spackling or if the wall is stained or discolored. If the repair work or stains are minor, you may just have to go around with a brush and spot prime these places. Any area that should be primed but isn't will show through when your paint dries.

Because your trim is essentially wood, the preparatory techniques are not exactly the same as for a wall. Getting the woodwork into shape can

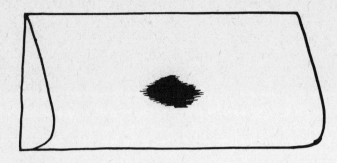

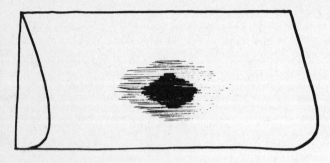

*piece of trim with paint chipped
off and the same piece sanded*

be a simple half-hour job if the house is new or very well preserved. If, like ours, it suffered abuse from a string of too many families and most recently from 4 St. Bernards, you have quite a job in store. For all wood, however, you begin in the same way.

a.) Check carefully for spots where old paint has chipped off. Using first a coarse or medium grade of sandpaper and then a finer grade, smooth down the damaged areas. At this point, the way it feels as you run your fingers along the sanded spot is more important than how it looks.

b.) Then check for scratches and gashes in the wood. Scratches can be sanded down as long as they are not so deep that your surface becomes concave from the sanding. For deep marks, you will have to use wood fill if you want a polished job. When you know, however, that a bed is going to cover that area forever and ever, you may decide to skip this step.

c.) When you have finished the sanding and have cleaned up all the dust, go around, paintbrush in hand, and prime the spots that you have worked on. Otherwise, the new paint won't look smooth and uniform.

d.) Be sure that the surface is not too glossy to accept a new coat of paint. When it is, the paint just refuses to go on evenly, and your surface begins to look like Swiss cheese. You can buy a liquid called "surface preparation" that goes on easily with a rag and which, when dry, makes the surface "tacky" enough for painting.

3. Organize the Room for the Job

Ideally, people like to paint the rooms of a house before they move into it. Realistically, we all know this is often impossible. If your room is filled with furniture, simply move as much of it as you can away from the walls, and cover everything with drop cloths. Paint really does splatter even when you don't realize it, depositing a fine mist of little dots over anything nearby, yourself included!

4. Paint the Surfaces

Since applying paint, regardless of the surface, depends on a small group of basic principles, let's examine them before we turn to the specific jobs.

Most rooms require the use of both roller and brushes. Rollers are best used to cover large surfaces like walls and ceilings. They consist of the roller itself and its sleeve or cover. Different sleeves are manufactured for oil-based and latex paint and for specific finishes and textures. They also vary in quality and cost. Since a roller is made to be reused, under normal conditions, it pays to invest in a good one unless the job is one where you know you will be ruining the sleeve and throwing it away (when doing coarse work like painting a concrete basement floor).

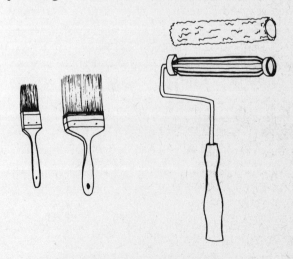

*sandbrush, squared typical
brush, roller sleeve, roller*

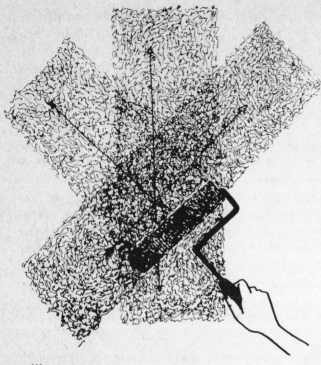

rolling process

Although mini-rollers are available for corners and trim, we have found brushes more effective for such tasks. They can get into the cracks and natural indentations of wood floors better, too. Like rollers, they differ in kind and quality as well as size. The smaller or more delicate the job, the smaller the brush you should use. Brushes also come tapered and square tipped. As you can imagine, a squared-off brush is good for flat surfaces, and tapered brushes are used for the smaller, narrower areas. Even more than with rollers, buying a good brush is a worthwhile investment if you take care of it. Cheap brushes lose bristles and don't produce a smooth, even finish.

Paint stores also abound with all sorts of gimmickry for the amateur (certainly no professional would go near them). Foam rubber on a stick or a piece of venetian blind with a handle to do edges are just two of the latest novelty items on the market. Try them if your sales resistance is low, but you will probably return to the trusty brush and roller in the end.

When the time comes to pick up the roller or brush for the first time, you'll need a firm command of the following basic techniques.

For Using a Roller
a.) Dip the roller into the pan which you have filled about halfway with paint.

b.) Roll off the excess on the slanted surface at the front of the pan.

c.) Bring the roller to your starting point, and begin by directing your roller up and down, then out to the right and back to the center, followed by the same stroke to the left and back, as indicated in the diagram. Then quickly go up and down over the whole area.

d.) Continue that pattern until the entire surface is covered, and there are no ridges of excess paint.

For Using a Brush
a.) Dip the brush only about halfway into the container. To conserve paint, you might also pour some into a smaller can or bucket.

b.) Wipe off excess paint along the side of the can or bucket to avoid dripping.

c.) Apply the paint in an up and down or back and forth motion. The wide side of the brush is used for larger areas and the thinner top edge for straight lines and narrow areas.

d.) Use different sized brushes for different areas, if you choose. A professional painter can paint a thin, straight line with a relatively thick brush, but we found this very difficult and had to use a thin artist's brush for such work.

For Using the Paint
a.) Stir continually, first before you start and then periodically during the job.

b.) Thin the paint when necessary with a bit of water or mineral spirits (depending on your paint).

c.) Keep the can's rim free of paint. If the rim fills up, paint will eventually drip down the can and splatter when you close it. The remainder will harden in the rim later and prevent the can from closing properly.

d.) Close the can whenever it is not in use. Even if you take a short break, the cover should go on. When you are ready to close up shop for the day, place the lid on the can, cover it with a rag to avoid splattering, and hammer the can closed.

Now you are really ready to paint! Follow these instructions for the specific areas to be covered.

Ceiling

The ceiling used to be an intimidating job,

guaranteed to leave the painter with a stiff neck. When someone invented the roller extension, though, everything changed. You can either use a broomstick, or a pole designed specifically for the job which can screw into your roller handle. Today all rollers are made to accommodate the threads of an extension pole. The only time you will have to get on a ladder is to paint the edges where ceiling meets wall—a roller cannot get that close.

a.) Take a 2″ or 3″ brush, a small amount of paint, and a damp rag with you as you move your ladder into the starting position.

b.) Paint a border of 2″ to 3″ around the edges of the entire ceiling, making sure the paint is spread smoothly and evenly. Do the same around the light fixture, if there is one. The rag you have brought up is available to catch any dribbles.

c.) Clean your brush.

d.) Fill your roller tray.

e.) Cover your head to protect it from the mist that is bound to fall.

f.) Starting from a corner, begin the rolling process described earlier. Get as close as you can to the edges to blend the brush work with the roller paint.

g.) Continue the rolling until the ceiling is finished.

Walls

Experts do not agree on the next surface to tackle; some of them say that the proper way is to do the walls after the ceiling, while other insist on doing the trim first. We have even heard of painters who coat the trim once, then do the walls completely, and finally apply a second coat to the trim at the end. By trial and error, we found ourselves getting better results by doing the walls first. Because we used some of the darker shades that are popular, we found that there was too much splatter onto the white trim when we did the trim first. When you do the walls remember this:

a.) Paint a 2″ to 3″ border around all edges first, as you did with the ceiling.

b.) Begin blending the border into the rest of the wall with the roller. If you have enjoyed working with the roller extension, start with it at the top, but complete one whole section (about 3′ wide) from top to bottom before moving along the wall.

c.) Check each section for drips or other imperfections before you go on.

Trim

Well-painted trim—doors, windows, and moldings—can really make a difference in a room, but this is the most difficult kind of surface to do. It also takes much longer than it would seem to finish the job. In area, it is miniscule compared to the ceiling and walls, but it is very delicate and often frustrating work.

The major difficulties are painting smoothly over areas that might still be glossy from previous paint, getting into all the grooves and curves found especially on the woodwork in older homes, and painting smooth lines to separate the wood from the walls or glass.

The first problem can be remedied by applying a surface preparation liquid to the wood, as we mentioned earlier. The detail work found on trim can be done most effectively by using the top edge of a tapered brush to get into all the little grooves. But no easy solution can be offered here for painting the straight line along the edges where the trim ends and another surface begins. Of course, a steady hand helps, and so does a patient nature. What doesn't work, we have found, is the application of tape to the window, floor, ceiling, or wall which is supposed to mask the area and serve as a guideline for your brush. Applying the tape takes hours, and getting it perfectly flush to the trim is no easy task. Even then, paint can still seep through, and afterward you often face great difficulty in removing it.

Basically, then, we find that using a variety of small, stiff brushes in combination with a rag (dampened with water or mineral spirits, depending on your paint) is best. Use a rag, wrapped around a fingernail, to smooth out a line. When the trim borders a wall, you'll have to allow the trim to dry, and then use wall paint to cover over any mistakes made from the other side. With windows, if your brush goes astray, let the paint dry, and the next day use a window scraper to remove the excess.

Floors

Interior floors are not often painted although they can make a room look quite outstanding, especially when patterns are then stenciled on them, something that is becoming popular today.

Second Coats

A painted floor almost always requires two coats to insure durability, but other surfaces may also need to be painted twice. When changing a color scheme from light to dark or dark to light, for example, one coat just won't cover regardless of how careful you are. So don't be surprised or dismayed if, after the first has dried, you have to return for a second round.

Cleaning Your Equipment

If you have used a water-based paint:

1.) Get as much excess paint out of the brush or roller before you put it under water by wiping it back and forth over newspaper.

2.) Take the brush or roller to your "work" sink, and run it under lukewarm water for a very long time. Try to work the paint out of the brush by bending it back and forth against the bottom of the sink and from the roller by rubbing your hand back and forth over the nap. You should do this until the water runs clean; have patience because this process will take a while.

3.) When the brush or roller is clean, remove excess water, and either hang it, if possible, or lay it flat to dry.

4.) Your roller tray, paint bucket, and rag should also be washed out with water whenever you clean your brush and roller.

If you have used an oil-based paint:

1.) Get as much excess paint from the brush as you can before you use any solvent by stroking it back and forth over newspaper.

2.) Then soak it in the cheapest kind of mineral spirits (the traditional way).

3.) You can also follow a quicker and more economical method. Take a whole newspaper, hold the brush on it, pour a little bit of mineral spirits over it, and work the spirits into the brush by wiping it back and forth on the paper. Continue the process by turning to the next page of paper, pouring on a bit more of the spirits and working it through. Keep at it until the brush wipes clean.

4.) Hang the brush or lay it flat to dry.

5.) If you have used a roller with oil-based paint, you can clean it, but it is very difficult, takes endless mineral spirits, and is very sloppy work. You may find it wiser to throw it away.

6.) Any other equipment that you have used for oil-based paint should be cleaned out, after each use, with mineral spirits.

7.) If you discover, after a brush has dried, that you accidentally did not clean it well enough, there are commercial brush cleaners sold which do work well for either oil or latex paint even if the brushes are in really bad shape.

Chapter 8

Floors

WOOD FLOORS

Overview

1.) Correct the sags.

2.) Replace or repair any damaged floorboards.

3.) Rent the floor sander, edger, and sandpaper.

4.) Sand down the inner surfaces of the floors with the drum sander in three stages (rough, medium, fine).

5.) Sand down the outer perimeter of the floor with the edger in three stages (rough, medium, fine).

6.) Thoroughly and spotlessly clean the entire floor.

7.) Apply the stain (usually in two coats).

8.) Apply the finish (in two or more coats).

First Considerations

There is something special and uniquely satisfying about the sight of a carefully finished wood floor. Anyone who appreciates the quality of fine wood knows that the most outstanding feature of a house could easily be its golden, wide-beamed oak floors.

Here, especially, homes built fifty or more years ago are likely to have a decided edge in quality. But you have to know the potential value of what you are looking at. No mistake is more fatal than to sigh in despair at the sight of a beat-up, faded wood floor and then decide that carpeting is your only recourse. You will sweat a bit before the floor is restored to your satisfaction, but you'll be glad you took the trouble. Unless the wood is hopelessly rotted or decrepit, there is a way to restore its former beauty.

We took no special notice of the floors when we first sized up the particulars of our house. The beams were wide, much wider than those of the floors we had grown up with, but they were pitted and lustreless, and in the early months of our ownership we gave them little thought. But when an oriental rug caught our eye, we abandoned the idea of wall-to-wall carpeting and decided to give floor refinishing a try.

If you are willing to take the plunge yourself, it is time to take stock of several important check points:

Does the floor sag noticeably? If it does, you had best start here by installing jack posts in the basement (not that difficult a job). If the trouble exists on the second floor, you obviously cannot place two attractive steel poles in the center of your living room or dining room. Your only recourse here is a professional contractor.

Are there a number of damaged floor boards that need to be repaired or replaced? This job should be seen to, as well, before you do any refinishing.

If you are certain that a very large area rug will be a permanent part of the room's decor, can you get away with sanding down the outer perimeter of the room *only*, leaving unfinished the inside section that will be covered by the rug?

Materials

To Correct Sags
- Piece of lumber to use as a straight edge
- Level

- Steel jack posts
- Pencil
- Concrete
- Trowel
- Nails

To Repair a Floor Board
- Wood filler (natural)
- Old chisel or screwdriver
- Electric sander with medium and coarse
  sandpaper

To Replace a Floor Board
- New piece of lumber
- Ruler
- Pencil
- Drill with ½" bit
- Chisel
- Hammer
- Finishing nails
- Nailset
- Wood filler

To Sand the Floor
- Drop cloths
- Drum sander, edger, and extension cord
  (rentals)
- Three grades of sandpaper for each machine
- Hammer
- Nailset

To Stain and Seal the Floor
- Stain/sealer
- Soft, clean rags
- Old toothbrush
- Newspaper
- Rubber gloves
- Mineral spirits

To Apply the Finish
- Polyurethane
- Brush
- Turpentine
- Fine grade sandpaper

Steps

1. Correct the Sags

How do you know whether or not your floor sags? Examine it carefully. The naked eye can usually detect a problem, but if you are uncertain, get a long straight edge (a good-sized piece of lumber will do) and fasten a level on top of it. Properly placed, the trapped bubble inside will indicate the sag by coasting off center.

Go to a lumberyard or hardware store, and buy the required number of adjustable steel jack posts in the appropriate sizes (they are available anywhere from 4' to 8'4"). Bring them down to the basement, and locate the precise area under the lowest point of the sag on the floor upstairs. Someone can help by lightly tapping on the proper spot from above. Mark this point with a pencil downstairs by placing an "X" on the girder (not the subfloor boards).

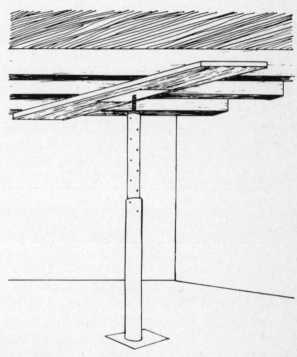

jack post

Now look at the basement floor below you, and make sure that it is thoroughly firm and solid. It is going to have to support considerable weight, so if your home is quite old, and the cellar floors are dirt, dig a 2' x 1½' rectangle to a depth of about 18", fill with concrete, trowel smooth, and allow to dry before you install the post. If, on the other hand, the basement floor is already concrete, but you find that the cement is chipped and crumbly, dig out the loose pieces and apply fresh concrete. Again, allow to dry before you proceed.

Most jack posts sold today are more less uniformly constructed. They consist of two steel tubes, one of which fits neatly into the other. The inside pole has a series of holes spaced at close intervals, through which a metal pin can be inserted in order to set the unit at a desired height. Finally, the screw jack top, which is built into the end of the inner tube, can be adjusted up or down (much the same as an automobile jack) to fit the entire apparatus at exactly the right level.

Here is what you should do:

a.) Position the base plate on the floor directly under the girder at the point you've previously marked off.

b.) Raise the inner tube so you can establish the nearest adjustment point without rising above the height of the girder. (In our case, the girder did not rest snugly against the upper plate of the jack post, so we set a 6″ x 1″ block of wood between the two and later drove heavy nails through all three to prevent slippage.)

c.) Rotate the jack screw until the upper plate comes into light contact with the girder.

Do not apply anything close to heavy pressure at this point.

d.) Get a level and check to see that the post is resting securely in place at an exact 90° angle to the girder. Adjust if necessary.

e.) Nail or bolt the girder to the top plate of the post. This will keep the whole structure firm. If you have rested a block of wood between the plate and the beam, nail all three together.

f.) Turn the jack up *slowly* so that a gentle pressure is applied against the girder. Now do nothing for at least twenty-four hours.

g.) Once a full day has passed, move the jack up still further to increase the pressure on the beam. You should be able to detect leveling of the floor in the room above at this point. But don't get impatient. Again, wait twenty-four hours before proceeding any further.

h.) Make the final upward adjustment of the jack, and check upstairs with a level. Be very careful not to tighten the jack so much that the floor begins to arch upward. A convex surface is no more desirable than a sagging one.

We cannot overstress the necessity to be patient between upward adjustments of the jack mechanism. Too quick an adjustment may cause severe problems of all kinds—the very frame of the house can suffer undue stress, and supporting beams can rupture.

2. Repair or Replace Any Damaged Floor Boards

When considering whether or not a particular piece of floor board needs to be replaced, remember that the damage has to be fairly extensive; most minor imperfections will be smoothed away in the sanding process, and deeper holes and cracks can generally be wood filled. Some sources recommend putty or paste epoxy for this purpose.

If wood filling is the best remedy:

a.) Buy a *natural color* wood filler, and apply a single layer to the gash with an old chisel, or even a wide blade screwdriver. Some brands do come in colors, but we've had only limited success trying to achieve a match.

b.) Allow this to dry, and then build up successive layers until the surface is level with the adjacent boards.

c.) Sand the final application smooth either by hand or machine. The drum sander will finish off the job for you. Don't worry about the color discrepancy. You will doubtless be staining the surface after sanding, and the filler will absorb the color along with the wood itself. There will always be some disparity in the resulting shades, since wood fillers vary in their ability to absorb stain, but these differences will blend perfectly well with the light and dark tones of the wood grain.

When a board is damaged beyond repair, though, wood filling won't do the trick. You'll need to remove the board and replace it. The delicate stage in this operation doesn't lie in the mechanics of removing the board and setting a new one in its place; it's in matching the old wood with a passable modern equivalent at your local lumber yard.

By far the most commonly used lumber in the construction of all hardwood floors is oak. If your home is more than fifty years old, though, they may have used something more unusual like walnut, cherry, maple, or pecan. It won't do to replace this with just anything. Add to that the problem of finding a suitable width, thickness, and texture, and you have an extended treasure hunt ahead of you.

There is no simple, direct route to the right source. Obviously, the best find would be random lengths of old wood, perhaps picked up at a junk-yard or salvage company, or even buried some-where in your basement. These will blend much better with the old boards than will new wood. Otherwise, shop around, using the telephone and making impromptu stops at local lumber yards. By all means remove the offending board first (directions on this follow soon), and keep the pieces temporarily in the back seat of your car.

Here is the simple procedure to follow to remove the old board and install the replacement:

a.) Mark off the damaged board with a car-penter's square or ruler.

b.) Using a power or hand drill fitted with a ½" bit, drill holes into all four corners of the board. Take care not to bore too deeply, or you will begin drilling into the subfloor.

c.) Get a chisel and hammer, and split the board lengthwise, again being careful not to make contact with the subfloor.

d.) Gently pry out the two pieces of the old board with the chisel and hammer.

e.) Measure very carefully, and then cut the replacement piece to the required fit.

f.) Notice that these floor boards are cut tongue and groove. This means that each strip has a "tongue" on one side which nestles comfortably into an adjacent board's "groove."

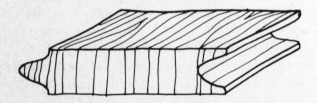

tongue and groove

To set in the new piece, you'll have to remove the lower portion of its groove with a chisel. Here's how the result should look.

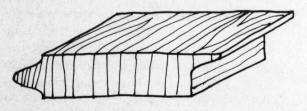

tongue and groove without lower half of groove

g.) Lower the board in at a 45° angle, fitting its tongue into the nearest neighbor's groove, and then slide the piece into place.

h.) Secure the board with finishing nails at all four corners, countersink, and wood fill the four holes.

i.) Finally, clear the room of as much furniture and bric-a-brac as possible, and cover anything that remains with a dropcloth.

3. Rent the Drum Sander, Edger, and Sandpaper Shopping Suggestions

There's no way to refinish a wood floor without renting the monstrously heavy drum sander and edger that are now standard equipment for the job. You need a strong back to brave this.

The best possible source for these machines is a tool rental agency. Use the telephone first to com-pare prices, but our guess is that you won't find too much variation. Check to make sure how much time is covered by the rental period. The place we used quoted us rates for a half day and a full day. You will probably wind up taking the full day unless you have a postage stamp floor to refinish. As a first timer, you'll be certain to need it since there is no such thing as a job that runs smoothly and according to schedule.

To compute the correct time allotment for any home improvement task you undertake, logically estimate how many hours the job will require, and then triple the result.

Make sure that the rental people explain in patient detail what safety precautions you should observe in using the machines. These monsters have a frisky habit of springing surprises on the unwary. Also find out what kind of electrical cur-rent the machine demands. Since it draws a lot of juice, your wiring must be strong enough for the job. Finally make sure that they have provided you with everything you need for the sanding process: three grades of sandpaper (coarse, medium, and fine), heavy duty extension cords, the two machines, and full instructions on their operation.

4. Sand Down the Inner Surfaces of the Floor

Read everything through before you start work. You should now have all the sanding equipment up the front steps and close at hand. The first machine you'll be using is the drum sander which will take care of the large inside surface.

a.) Load it with the coarsest grade of sandpaper according to instructions.

b.) *IMPORTANT:* Before you move the sander onto the floor area, take a hammer and nailset into the room, and carefully comb every single board to make sure there are no protruding nail heads. These have a way of ripping nastily into the sandpaper and tearing it to shreds without warning.

c.) Making sure the power switch is off, plug in the machine, and move it into place at the starting position. Tilt the whole unit up at 45° angle so that it won't run away from you when it's first activated, and then turn the power switch to "on."

d.) Now you are going to move forward across the full length of the floor, *with* the grain of the wood, until you reach the other side of the room. Lower the machine slowly, slowly, until the sandpaper comes into contact with the floorboards.

e.) Immediately begin walking straight ahead AT A SLOW, EVEN PACE. This is the single most important direction to observe. We weren't especially careful here the first time, and the results showed it.

f.) When you reach the other side, again tilt the machine to a 45° angle to prevent it from cutting too deeply into the outer edges. Make a complete turn on the wheels, and face the direction from which you started, this time setting the sander down right next to and slightly overlapping the path you've just travelled. Continue walking back and forth in exactly this way until you finish the entire inside surface of the floor.

g.) Check periodically to determine how much more sawdust the vacuum bag can swallow. It has a tendency to fill up faster than you might guess.

h.) The rental shop will probably give you three or more pieces of each grade of sandpaper. As soon as you sense that the machine is no longer cutting efficiently into the wood, look to see whether the old paper needs to be replaced.

You may wonder, as we did, whether you need to remove every trace of the original stain from the surface and restore the pure color of the natural wood. Or is taking most of it off sufficient? The answer depends on the result you're working for. If the former occupants left you with dark floors, and you plan to refinish the wood this time in a blond tone, naturally, you will have to remove all the old color, perhaps with the added help of a vibrating hand sander to finish off the few stubborn spots. But if the color of the stain you want to apply is about the same or darker than the original, don't worry about the few traces of color your sander may leave behind.

i.) Once you've been across the entire inside surface with the coarse sandpaper, repeat the process, in exactly the same order, with the medium sandpaper, and then the fine sandpaper.

5. Sand Down the Outer Perimeter of the Floor

It's time for the edger. Proceed with care because you're going to feel a little less lively now than when you began.

a.) Fit the machine with the coarse grade of sandpaper as per instructions, but before you start, move to a remote corner, perhaps where a large piece of furniture will later rest, and try it out.

Good news! It's 25% of the weight of the first machine, and consequently much easier to work with.

Bad news! The sheet of sandpaper which covers the metal disc travels in a circular motion, so if you're not careful to apply an even pressure, you may wind up with circular scars in the floor.

b.) Once you've mastered the touch, forge ahead. Cover the entire perimeter of the floor with the machine, first with the coarse, then the medium, then the fine paper. Don't skip any of these steps out of laziness or fatigue as we did. You'll regret it later. For the one, tiny inaccessible spot in all four corners, you will have to resort to good old hand held paper. When everything is finished to your satisfaction, return the equipment to the rental outlet.

6. Thoroughly and Spotlessly Clean the Entire Floor

Apart from an accumulation of stray chips of wood, the floor will now be covered with a thin blanket of sawdust. Use your own heavy duty vacuum cleaner to take care of the residue, and finish up with a dustpan.

Don't miss window ledges or any other surfaces above the floor that might have gathered dust. Also, try at all costs not to step on the floors once they've been cleaned. The pores in the grain are all wide open and especially vulnerable at this stage.

7. Apply the Stain

This was the step we looked forward to since it was supposed to have been the easiest. Through experience, we should have known better.

The first minor confusion we met was trying to distinguish between the terms *stain* and *sealer*. The books on floor refinishing are often careless about defining the differences.

A *stain* is simply a pigment in liquid form which gives a desired color to the wood without concealing the beautiful natural grain.

A *sealer* (the best kind is called penetrating resin sealer) is also a liquid which you must spread over the floor after staining to seal (close) the pores in the wood. Without a sealer, the final finish (shellac, varnish, polyurethane, etc.) will sink into the wood instead of remaining on the surface which is where it should stay.

Confusion arises because most modern stains you buy (Minwax, for example) already contain a sealer and so enable you to combine two steps into one.

Of course, if the color of the wood after sanding is exactly what you want in the finished floor, you need not use any stain at all but would instead apply a sealer and then two coats of either paste wax, shellac, varnish, or polyurethane.

A product called *varnish stain*, on the other hand, allows you to execute all three steps in one shot—sealing of the pores, staining, and finishing. STAY AWAY FROM THIS MATERIAL. It will cover up the grain much like paint and harden to a cheap-looking, sticky gloss.

Nothing should be easier than applying the stain/sealer. Although instructions for various brands may differ slightly, the basic procedure is as follows:

a.) Get together a soft clean rag (a piece of lintfree bedsheet is ideal), an old toothbrush, some newspaper, and the gallon of stain in the color you've selected. Always test a small amount first, to make sure the shade is right.

b.) Put on some old pants and rubber gloves, and, remembering to keep the floor absolutely clean, set your gear down at the furthest corner of the room, and spread out some newspaper.

c.) Dip the rag into the stain, and rub it vigorously into the wood surface, moving evenly

two people stripping one floor

result of two people staining one floor

back and forth and rubbing with the grain. Go over areas that you miss whenever you catch them. Use the toothbrush dipped in stain to get at the difficult spots.

d.) Continue in just this way until you've covered the entire surface, moving the newspaper and equipment along with you as you go. Work with an even touch, and keep the amount of liquid on your rag relatively constant.

e.) When you've gone over the whole floor, the job may be finished right there, although a second coat will be needed if you want a darker color. If so, wait twenty-four hours and simply repeat the whole process.

f.) If the second coat is too dark, dip a rag in mineral spirits and rub lightly over the entire floor.

When two people are staining one floor, two different shades may result. The solution is not simply to go over the entire right half of the floor with one more coat to compensate for the disparity. The trouble does not lie in matching the color of the right half of the floor with the left at all. It's that center line indicated by the arrows where the two participants' handiwork meet.

That line caused us long hours of anxiety. Try as we might, lightly brushing on turpentine, light-ly blending in stain, lightly dabbing with rags, steel wool and Q-Tips, the ghost of a very perceptible line down the center of the dining room floor stubbornly remained.

We decided to stop agonizing over the whole thing, leave it as is, and hope the coats of finishing material would magically erase the line for us. Eventually this is just what happened, though neither of us has ever been able to figure out why.

8. Apply the Finish

A finish is applied over the coats of fully dried stain to protect the wood and add lustre. Although it is possible to omit this step, it is not a good idea. Not only is a stain/sealer insufficient protection against wear, but whenever moisture later comes into contact with the floorboards, you run the risk of taking up some of the stain.

Unfortunately, the choices are extremely numerous. We had no idea what qualities made shellac different from varnish, varnish different from polyurethane. (Forget about lacquer. That's for furniture refinishing only!) In addition, there is the matter of shine to consider: do you want a matte finish, a satin finish, a semi-gloss, a high gloss?

We are going to help you eliminate all this confusion right away by expressing a definite preference for polyurethane varnish. It has significant advantages over shellac, wax, and traditional varnish both in ease of application and durability. The difference between it and plain old varnish is that polyurethane is a modern synthetic material which yields a waxlike finish minus the wax, can be maintained more easily than any of the other finishes, and is supremely resistant to stains and scratches.

Polyurethane can generally be bought in any of three varieties: high gloss or glossy (for a very bright sheen similar to the look of a gym or bowling alley floor); satin or semi-gloss (some glow, but without the glasslike shine typical of high gloss); and flat or matte finish (no gloss to speak of). Your decision here is purely a matter of taste. Here is the process:

a.) Stir (don't shake) the can thoroughly.

b.) Brush the polyurethane over a piece of scrapwood. If the brush drags, you should probably dilute the liquid *slightly* with turpentine.

c.) Apply to the floor, keeping the brush fully loaded, and working in long, even sweeps, overlapping as you go. Be very careful not to allow lint or dust to settle into the finish (if it does, a bit of softened resin stuck to the end of a stick will remove it cleanly). In any case, close off the area from any drafts.

d.) Allow to dry according to the manufacturer's instructions (usually overnight for best results).

e.) Sand by hand *very lightly* and wipe away dust.

f.) Apply a second coat, allowing sufficient drying time.

g.) Naturally, if the directions on the can conflict with these steps at all, you should do as they say.

This kind of floor requires no waxing and should be maintained simply by regular cleaning with a slightly dampened sponge mop.

We have visited homes in which the floors were professionally finished with polyurethane varnish, and the homeowners cursed the results. We never had this problem, but there are only three possible explanations: insufficient drying time between the coats, the choice of a high gloss polyurethane (as opposed to satin or matte) which always shows up scratch marks more readily, undue stress on a newly finished floor, such as a hoard of frolicking children or scraping furniture around two days after the finishing job has been completed.

Paint

There are only two valid reasons (in our view) for resorting to paint over a natural wood floor. One is if your floor is in an out-of-the-way upstairs bedroom and is in such dreadful shape as to make the refinishing process a basically thankless effort. If that is the case, you would probably sand and woodfill to whatever degree your energy and patience allowed, apply two coats of floor or deck paint, wait for it to dry, and then place furniture or area rugs over strategic spots to conceal imperfections.

The other consideration is aesthetic. If there are wood floors in every other room of your house, you may feel motivated to paint one of them just for variety or in order to obtain a certain decorative effect.

Make sure, if you're using a white paint which the manufacturer specifically recommends for floors, that the color is not appreciably different from the color white you are using for moldings or trim in the same room. You'd be amazed how significantly tints of white can differ.

Do not choose a color like white for a floor that will have to bear up under heavy traffic. As you might expect, it shows dirt readily.

Linoleum Floors

We are wood floor enthusiasts, but for practical use over any well-travelled area, they aren't exactly ideal. In the kitchen, bathroom, or foyer, you will probably want to use either linoleum, vinyl tile, ceramic tile, or even slate (of course, there are other possibilities as well).

Our consideration of linoleum (or any other sheet materials) won't take very long. Don't try it. It is easy enough to plot the installation on paper, but when your body comes up against those unwieldy 6' widths, you will curse the whole venture, and we will say we told you so. Large quantities of glue need to be spread at a time, the edges must be precut to conform perfectly with any irregularites in the perimeter of the room, and the sections have to be rolled flat to the undersurface with enormous pressure to achieve a lasting bond. Of course, we were warned repeatedly to leave this or that renovation chore to the pros and went ahead despite all the well meant advice, so you'll have to discover your own limitations.

VINYL TILES

Overview

1.) Measure the room to decide how much tile you need.
2.) Purchase the required tile.
3.) Gather the necessary materials.
4.) Prepare the existing surface.
5.) Set up a trial layout of the tiles.
6.) Apply the adhesive and install the tiles.
7.) Cut and install the irregular tiles.

First Considerations

When we moved into our house, the kitchen was in far better shape than any other room. Until an early visitor to the house remarked "Lovely old place, but what are you going to do with that awful kitchen floor?" we had not even given any thought to the need for a new one. In fact, our immediate instinct was to ask the lady where she came off. Then we looked at the floor again, exchanged that familiar resigned look, and set ourselves to work.

Our first choice, oddly enough after what we said before, was linoleum. The no-wax varieties (which turn out to need upkeep after all) were then very popular and came in some rather attractive patterns. We soon learned that this choice would be impractical, though, since the room was large, and we had so few skills.

Thus we decided to try individual solid vinyl tiles instead, something we thought we could manage on our own. We saw two advantages to the tiles: first, if we started out and found we couldn't handle the job, all we would have wasted were a few 12″ x 12″ pieces before we hired someone to finish the work; secondly, if there was a spot where a tile buckled, we could simply remove and replace a small area.

We had a harder time finding patterns that pleased us, but if you are willing to invest in the better and more expensive solid vinyl, the styles can be quite attractive and will last infinitely longer than linoleum or the cheaper vinyl or vinyl asbestos tiles.

Shopping Suggestions

Comparison shopping does pay off when you're looking for floor tiles. Most stores offer a variety of qualities and brands, but the price tags on the same items may vary. You might start out by going to a store that has a large selection, regardless of cost, and when you find something you like, shop around for the best price.

If you are intent upon getting the best for the least, you may want to investigate the possibility of buying "seconds." A second will have some flaw, but it may be slight or virtually unnoticeable. We got our tile directly from a distributor who was a friend of the family. He suggested that we buy some seconds for the less visible areas of the room in order to save money.

Materials

- Assorted rags
- Mineral spirits
- Tiles
- Adhesive
- Brush, sawtooth trowel, or roller
- Carpenter's square
- Heavy duty, well-sharpened scissors
- Pencil or suitable marker
- Ruler or yardstick

Steps

Prepare the Existing Surface

In our bathroom, we removed the vinyl tile before putting down a ceramic floor, but our kitchen floor seemed more solid. We took a gamble and won; the floor has been trouble free from the beginning and promises to remain so. You'll have to use some good sense here.

If the floor you're starting with is wood, the boards should be planed down in the high spots if necessary and smoothed with a sander. Then lay masonite or plywood over it for an even undersurface.

If you're starting with linoleum or old vinyl asbestos tiles, you should be able to lay the new floor right over it, provided it's in good solid contact with the subfloor. A loose or uneven bond won't do. This doesn't mean that the old floor has to *look* good, but that it must lay flat and firm. If it doesn't, you must either make it so, or rip it up.

In any case, detailed instructions for preparing an existing surface for tiling can be found in the chapter on ceramic tile.

Set Up a Trial Layout of the Tiles

This is the stage where you will be eager to begin spreading adhesive and covering up the old tiles with the handsome new ones. Not quite yet. If you began in the center of the room and started installing the tiles in a perpendicular row, you might find yourself caught at one end or the other with only two or three inches of space remaining. This is a bad idea, not only because such a thin width looks strange, but because the job of cutting off so narrow a piece of tile is impossibly awkward. To avoid that pitfall, you will begin instead with a quick dry run.

a.) Clear the room of all possible furniture and remove the baseboard moldings.

b.) Take a yardstick and locate the midpoint of one wall.

c.) Using your square, extend this point out across the floor at a perfect 90° angle, either with pencil or chalk.

d.) Locate the midpoint of this line, and again using the square, draw a second line perpendicular to the first. Extend it out to touch the two remaining walls.

If you have one of those handy tools called a chalk line, you can make convenient use of it here instead of fumbling along with the yardstick.

Here's how the floor should now look:

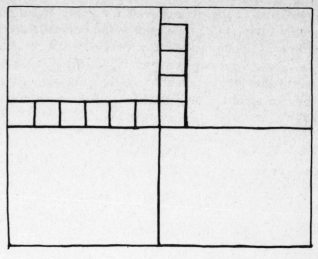

a cross of tiles

e.) *Without applying any adhesive at this point,* take a batch of tiles and arrange them along the lines you've just drawn. Stop as soon as it becomes impossible to fit a full tile in any of the four directions. This way, you'll be able to see if the dimensions of your room will leave you with any of those skinny rows. When this occurs just move the appropriate row up or down so that whatever space you're left with at both ends of the vertical row is practical for tile cutting.

The only other situation to avoid is allowing the spaces between the tiles to fall directly on a seam in the underlayment. With time, these seams are likely to expand slightly and encourage cracking of the tiles.

Not all rooms are perfect rectangles, of course. If the perimeter of your room is irregular, you may have to set down almost all the tiles before

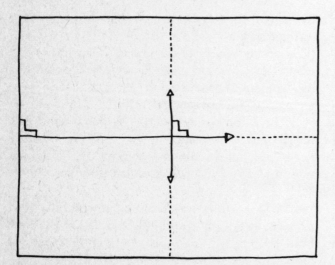

trial layout for tiles

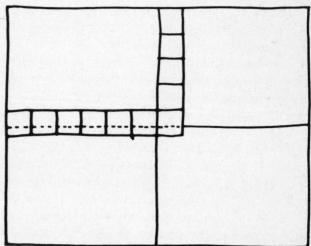

adjustment of tiles

gluing them to be sure that none of those narrow spaces turns up. If they do, make the appropriate adjustments. Also, remember that once the tiles are laid, you'll be replacing the baseboard moldings, so the fit doesn't have to be 100% snug.

3. Lay the Adhesive and Install the Tiles

Since floor tiles are manufactured in a wide assortment of materials, there is a correspondingly large variety of adhesives available for installing them. Today, the many brands fall into two basic categories: one is the texture of butterscotch pudding and gets put down in a thin coat with a sawtooth trowel; the other can simply be rolled or brushed onto the surface and is much easier to work with.

The important thing here is to buy the adhesive that is manufactured specifically for the tiles you're laying. Solid vinyl may require one kind, vinyl asbestos another, asphalt another. The wrong choice can be fatal.

a.) Carefully read the directions on whatever can of glue you've bought, and then, in accordance with these directions, set down a quantity of adhesive inside ONE of the four quadrants marked off by the lines you've drawn. You can fill that entire space if you want, somewhat less if you're doing a particularly large room. DON'T ALLOW THE ADHESIVE TO OBSCURE THE GUIDELINES YET.

b.) The adhesive directions sometimes specify a waiting time. If so, wait.

c.) Put down a single row of tiles along the guideline. Don't slide them into place; that may cause some adhesive to ooze up. Just lay them flat. Butt each successive tile to the one you've just laid. Be exacting here in order to ensure an even job.

d.) Once a single row is down, horizontally and vertically, you have automatically established your guidelines for the remainder of the floor. Just make sure that each successive tile is perfectly butted to its neighbor.

e.) Continue now to spread adhesive and install successive rows until all the full tiles have been laid.

f.) Now proceed in exactly the same way with the remaining three quadrants until you've laid down all the full, uncut tiles that will fit over the entire floor surface. Use your cut rags dipped in mineral spirits immediately whenever some stray

adhesive slips onto the tile surface. This is by far the easiest time to remove it. Don't worry too much about walking over these newly laid tiles, however. Once they're down, they shouldn't shift around.

Cut and Install the Irregular Tiles to Conform to the Outer Perimeter of Your Room

If a tile just needs cutting along one line, making it a narrower rectangle to fit in at the edges of the floor, the job is simple.
For Rectangular Shapes
a.) Preheat your oven to 300°.
b.) Bring a full tile over to the spot you're working on (it doesn't matter where you start) and place it directly over the last full tile you've glued in the row.
c.) Now take a *second* full tile and place it over the first one, BUT THIS TIME MOVE ITS EDGE FLUSH TO THE WALL.
d.) Draw a pencil line across the first loose tile, using the top tile as your guiding edge.
e.) Place the tile (you can actually do several at a time when you get more confident) into the oven for a few minutes to soften it and make it easier to cut across the line with a sharp scissors. Some people use clothes irons, blow torches, or the gas jets on top of the stove for this purpose, but we found the oven the least hazardous solution.
f.) Finally, remove the softened tile, cut across the line with your scissors, glue, and install it like any other tile. Again, remember that if your cut tile is just a bit imperfect, the moldings will conceal the mistakes.

If you must cut an irregular shape, you have to make a paper pattern very similar in method to the one described in the chapter on ceramic tiles. Use the following technique to cut a tile to fit around pipes, permanently installed cabinets, door frames, entrance ways, etc.
For Irregular Shapes
a.) Take a sheet of paper large enough to cover a full tile, and bring it to the spot where the irregular shaped tile will be installed. Butt it to the edge of the last full tile you've glued in.
b.) Using your index finger, press firmly against the contour of whatever irregular shape it is you're trying to reproduce.
c.) Take a scissors and cut the appropriate shape into the sheet of paper.
d.) Lay this over a full loose tile, and transfer

the irregular shape from the paper to the surface of the tile with your pencil. Don't make the mistake (easy to do) of letting the pattern run in the wrong direction when you transfer it to the tile.

e.) Place the tile into a 300° oven for a few minutes to soften it.

f.) Remove the tile, cut along the pencil line with your scissors, glue, and install.

As soon as you've cut and installed the last irregular tile, finish the job by replacing the baseboard molding.

Chapter 9

Decorating With Wood

FURNITURE REFINISHING

Overview

1.) Gather the necessary materials.
2.) Remove the old finish.
3.) Prepare the wood and smooth it thoroughly.
4.) Apply the stain/sealer.
5.) Apply the finish.

First Considerations

The process of restoring faded wood can be the most deeply satisfying of all the home renovating chores. Old furniture is deserving of your time and affection, no matter how scarred its superficial appearance. Furthermore, if the results are anything like you'd hoped they'd be, you'll know the satisfaction of having performed an act of honest craftsmanship.

But let's return to earth long enough to sound a stern warning: don't come to wood refinishing if you are the sort who needs instant gratification. This work is long and slow. It proceeds in gradual stages that are impossible to rush or skip over because the liquids you apply to the wood need to dry thoroughly before you can move to the next step. It's true that modern stains and finishes dry much more rapidly than the old ones did. But if you brush a coat of varnish onto a table early one Saturday, you're making a mistake by trying to sand it smooth before Sunday, no matter *what* the label on the can says (DRIES HARD IN ONE HOUR!). The material not only needs to dry, but to *set* completely. So the key to success is patience—a rich and inexhaustible supply.

If you've done any wood refinishing at all, you already know a fact kept secret from the rest of humanity: the most depressingly shabby piece of furniture can be restored, provided you train your eye to pick up its potential beauty and look ahead to the finished product. We've been exposed as amateurs more than once while browsing through antique stores with our parents. My father will stand longingly over a drab old curio cabinet that we would at best have considered for firewood. A few times he was so furious over our short-sightedness that he'd buy and refinish the piece just to show us up for fools. He would invariably score his point. But don't misunderstand us here: an undistinguished looking desk doesn't automatically become beautiful just because it's an antique. If it was ugly in 1908, it's going to be ugly today. In other words, make sure your goal is worthwhile before you decide to invest your time. So far we've made the investment four times, in each case to our thorough satisfaction: an oak china closet gunked up with cheap, glossy shellac that we found stuffed with yellowed papers in our parents' basement; a round lamp table with fluted edges whose graceful, curved lines were all but obscured beneath layers of dark red paint; (We picked it up for five dollars in a Vermont barn.) a small drop leaf writing desk that we bought in decent enough shape and then nearly ruined with two coats of opaque varnish stain; a so-called Hoosier cabinet for the kitchen—our most prized find—from which we stripped away generations of stubborn "milk paint." A dealer sold it to us "as is" for $35.00. We've seen them in every other local antique store recently for $300.00 and up.

Before you begin working, make sure you've charted your course wisely. Examine the piece of furniture you're about to restore. If it needs any kind of structural repairs—that is, if the upholstery is sagging, the joints are loose, or the legs broken—you have two choices: either get hold of a detailed text on furniture repair and acquire the necessary skills or (a more prudent decision for the rank beginner) bring it to a reliable professional. We're talking here about a highly skilled craft. If the piece is in good shape structurally, but the problems are with the finish, you have two choices again: either find out whether the original finish can be saved through cleaning away superficial layers of dirt and patching up individual blemishes, rings, or stains (again, consult the sort of text mentioned earlier), or strip away the old finish and start completely from scratch. As it happens, this last route is the one we travelled each and every time we got involved.

Shopping Suggestions

A stain is nothing more than a thinned down paint which you rub into the sanded wood if you want to alter its color. The natural tone of raw wood (what you find in unpainted furniture stores and what your own piece will probably resemble when you finish stripping it down) is not rich enough to satisfy most traditional tastes—although right now, the look is very much in vogue. If you use raw wood selectively, as we did in our kitchen, it can make for an effective contrast. But if you do want to deepen the color, a stain is the right thing to use.

Of the three kinds widely available—oil-based rubbing stains, non-grain raising stains, and water stains (packets of powder that you dissolve in very hot water)—we have used only the first type. It's a superior product with no evident drawbacks, and it comes in the widest choice of colors. Furthermore, with some brands—Minwax, for example—the shades can be blended freely in whatever proportions you like. That way you can play around with an assortment of custom tones and wind up with your own unique mixture. You'll find a large chart in the stores which displays several rows of sample wood chips, usually in pine or oak. These are supposed to let you see what the available colors will look like when you apply them to the particular wood you're working with. Don't place too much faith in these samples; we've had little success with them. Until you get to rub a few dabs into an inconspicuous corner of the actual piece you have at home, you'll never know what precisely to expect. Just hope the salesperson is cooperative about allowing you to return an unwanted can or two.

Materials

For Removing Paint or an Old Clear Finish
- A propane torch or sufficient quantity of liquid paint remover
- A supply of medium and coarse grades of steel wool (#2 and #3)
- A strong wire scrub brush
- An old paint brush and toothbrush for applying paint remover
- Various scrapers in several widths
- Lots of assorted rags, precut
- Plenty of old newspaper
- Several old coffee cans
- Rubber gloves
- Mineral spirits

For the Smoothing Process
- A power orbital sander
- A supply of sandpaper in both medium and fine grades
- Sandpaper blocks for whenever the paper needs to be hand held
- Wood glue (optional) for mixing with sawdust to build up gashes or holes
- Wood filler (if needed)
- Vacuum cleaner

For Staining
- A sufficient quantity of stain/sealer in your chosen color
- Assorted lint-free rags
- Old newspaper
- Mineral spirits
- Rubber gloves
- Old toothbrush

For the Finish
- A sufficient quantity of the desired finishing material and its solvent
- Brush
- Several fine grades of steel wool (#000 and #0000)
- Old newspaper

Steps

1. Remove the Old Finish

Once you've decided that stripping away the old finish is inevitable, you must prepare yourself for one of life's grimiest chores. Regardless of the method, you will be swimming in sludge, so give yourself over to the experience and have a good time. Before you start, slip into your most comfortable rags, spread out plenty of newspaper, and choose your weapons.

Once again there are a few practical choices. The most common one is to buy a gallon of liquid paint remover and brush it on in gradual stages, scraping away more of the old finish (whether it's paint, varnish, shellac, or whatever) with each application. Frankly, it's slow going. Another is the propane torch method. We've tried both of these, and, while the torch is infinitely quicker and simpler once you acquire the knack, we're not going to recommend it here for two reasons: it can start fires easily in the hands of a less than meticulous worker, and even cautiously used, if you accidentally hold it in one spot for too long, it can blacken the wood surface so that even prolonged sanding won't help. A third alternative now storming the market is the so-called "heat gun," which friends of ours have praised without reservation. There has been considerable controversy surrounding its use, however, and since we haven't ever tried one, we can't do much more than mention it. For the time being, then, stay with the liquid.

a.) Make sure to work in a well-ventilated area. Paint remover is strong stuff, and you don't want to inhale the fumes.

b.) Set the furniture over thick layers of old newspaper.

c.) Remove any hardware from the piece, and, if there are drawers, pull them and strip them down separately.

d.) Take an empty coffee can, and fill it about halfway full with paint remover.

e.) Work on the relatively large, flat surfaces first. Soak your brush in the paint remover, and lay it smoothly over a limited section. Apply it generously; you want to saturate the surfaces so that the liquid will penetrate deeply.

f.) Here's the key: wait at least ten solid minutes before you make another move. The chemical needs time to take effect, so if you begin scraping right away, you'll get only a fraction of its peak efficiency. Just before you begin the actual scraping, soak a new section so that it's ready to be removed after you've worked on the first area.

g.) Take your metal scraper, whichever size is most appropriate, and scrape away the old finish in long, even strokes. The idea is to get as much off at once as possible, not to chop and hack away at any particular spot. If the finish is giving you a hard time coming loose, stop immediately and brush on another thick coat of the paint remover. Wait a few minutes and then try again. Each time your scraper travels across the wood, wipe off any accumulated waste in a scrap of newspaper. Refill the coffee can as needed.

h.) Continue in just this way, working all the more accessible, flat surfaces first. You will find no matter how carefully you do the job or how thickly you've applied the remover, that some stubborn spots will resist the scraper. Don't go after these just yet. Take off the bulk of the old finish first, and go back and do the detail work later.

i.) Curved or ornately carved sections are more difficult to do. You brush on the liquid and let it penetrate just as before, but this time the removal process will be more time-consuming. It's best to handle these spots with a combination of techniques: dip some coarse steel wool in the remover and rub away; use your wire brush; try the toothbrush—whatever works best! No matter what the method, there will be certain places where the old finish will cling to the wood even after six tries. Patience, as we said.

j.) Once the rough work has been done, go back to those remaining spots and work them until the old finish has been completely removed. Naturally, if there are drawers or accessories, you'll need to go back and repeat the process.

k.) Pause here to let the furniture dry completely overnight. Then give it a generous coat of mineral spirits to remove any film or residue, and once again allow it to dry.

2. Prepare the Wood and Smooth It Thoroughly

You are ready for this step as soon as the piece has dried completely. The goal now is to remove as many flaws in the wood as possible before applying a stain and finish—chips, dents, scratches, etc. That, of course, means sanding all surfaces until they are as smooth as you can get them. Don't overdo it, though. Any deep imperfections that the sandpaper can't eliminate at this point will be fixed up later on.

a.) Use aluminum oxide or garnet paper, beginning with a medium grade and working down through fine and extra-fine. Don't take any short cuts here.

b.) The whole job can be managed with a hand held sanding block to which your paper has been stapled, but you'll have a much easier time if you work the large flat areas with a power orbital sander. Curved or delicately carved sections, though, must be done by hand, and preferably with your sandpaper attached to a curved block of wood that will allow for better contact with hard-to-reach areas.

c.) Remember to sand with the grain whenever possible.

d.) As soon as the sanding is finished to your satisfaction, you can work on the deeper flaws mentioned earlier. Either use the wood filler technique, or try this more resourceful method. Gather up a quantity of the sawdust from the sanding operation. Don't allow it to get dirty. Place this either on an old piece of plywood or a very large bottle top, and mix it with a small quantity of wood glue. How much? You'll have to feel as you go. This homemade wood filler paste is ideal for the patch job you're trying to do because its color is obviously identical to that of the piece of furniture itself. With plastic wood, such a match is next to impossible to achieve. Take a quantity of the mixture on a small scraper, and work it evenly into the hole or crevice. Continue until the surface is level and smooth. If you're patching a particularly deep spot, you may have to allow one layer to dry several hours and then build up the rest with one or more additional applications. Always over rather than underfill. When the material has dried completely, go over it with your orbital sander.

e.) For super smoothness, finish up with the finest grade of steel wool.

f.) Brush away and then vacuum up all traces of dust.

3. Apply the Stain/Sealer

A sealer is simply a coat of your chosen finish diluted in its own thinner. You brush this onto the wood after sanding to close the pores and prevent additional coats of finish from penetrating the surface. But if you are going to use a stain, applying this sealer may be unnecessary because many modern brands already *contain* the sealer. Check the label closely. If this is the case, you can proceed right away to the staining process itself, the techniques for which are precisely the same as for wood floors. Note, however, that in looking over the color of your wood after sanding, there's nothing that says you can't leave the piece just as is, especially if enough of the original stain has been retained to satisfy you. You may even decide to go one or two shades lighter—a simple matter of rubbing on coats of plain old undiluted laundry bleach. For both these choices, though, a sealer coat will be essential. Be sure the piece is entirely free of any dust or dirt by wiping with a tack rag— a smooth cloth soaked in water, wrung out and then wet with turpentine, wrung out again and dampened with varnish.

4. Apply the Finish

We assume if you are bothering to invest this much tender loving care on a piece of furniture that you will be interested in one of the clear finishes that doesn't conceal the beautiful natural wood grain. That rules out paint, antique glazes, and enamel, all of which you would resort to only if you didn't feel the natural wood was particularly worth displaying. Unfortunately that still leaves you with a bewildering range of possibilities: lacquer, natural resin varnish, polyurethane, shellac, boiled linseed oil, and scores of others. As with floors, we are convinced that polyurethane is your smartest choice. For purists, however, who demand a more classic finish, we also include here directions for achieving a rich hand-rubbed finish using antique oil.

To Apply Polyurethane
Consult the instructions on how to give a polyurethane finish to your wood floors. The process is exactly the same for furniture: once the stain/sealer has dried completely, brush on a coat of the polyurethane, wait a day, sand *very* lightly, brush on a second coat, wait a day, sand *very* lightly again, brush on a final coat. Some sources urge fine steel wool instead of sandpaper because it enables you to work with a lighter touch. The

only possible added caution you may need to observe in applying the polyurethane to furniture is to check the brush strokes constantly to make sure that small droplets of the finish aren't forming along the surfaces. Since you'll be working against gravity on all the vertical planes, this is always a good possibility.

To Apply Antique Oil

Antique oil will never give you the durability of a polyurethane finish, and the overall process is both longer and more painstaking, but you will end up with the kind of mellow, rich finish that will draw praise from the most discriminating elder craftsmen.

a.) Make certain the furniture is thoroughly dry. Place equal parts boiled linseed oil and turpentine in a large double boiler and heat the mixture. Be very cautious about fire—don't fill the pot too high.

b.) Brush on a wet, thick coat. Keep brushing on more until the wood will drink in no more.

c.) Allow to set for awhile; then wipe off the excess.

d.) After twenty-four hours, buff well with a soft lintfree cloth.

e.) Repeat the process immediately from steps 1 to 4 each day for a week.

f.) Thereafter, repeat every week for a month, every month for a year, and every year forevermore.

This is not an easy venture, but it's worth the effort if you demand a special soft lustre.

MOLDINGS

Overview

1.) Check over the condition of the moldings to determine your needs.
2.) Repair, smooth, and refinish any mendable holes and dents.
3.) Replace (or improvise replacements for) moldings that are damaged beyond repair.
4.) Measure, miter, and apply new moldings; then refinish.

First Considerations

The original moldings in an older home are probably the single best reflection of their era—an age in which people still had time for elegance and graceful detail. You won't find the same solid, handsomely crafted wood trim in today's lumberyards, as we were soon embarrassed to discover.

Checking over the condition of the moldings when we moved in was a brutal awakening. It was the first time we realized the full weight of what we were in for. Chips and dents were everywhere; that was the least of it. The paint had yellowed and cracked and was many layers thick; the 4 infamous St. Bernards had apparently been encouraged to dine on the woodwork since several areas were chewed up beyond recognition; a full wall's worth in the living room had disappeared completely to be replaced by straight lengths of 1" x 6" lumber! Where to begin?

We adopted and discarded a variety of approaches and invested more of our time here than we did anywhere else in the house. On one misguided afternoon, we even set forth on a plan to blowtorch away all ninety years of accumulated paint and restore the natural wood moldings completely. Four hours later, after successfully stripping away *half* the wood trim surrounding our front door, we stopped to reclaim our sanity.

Unless you want the renovation of a house to occupy your every waking moment, stripping down the wood trim is not terribly practical. The purist in you may be tempted, but we predict that you'll lose your mind somewhere along the way.

Materials

For Repairing Damaged Moldings
- Assorted grades of sandpaper
- Power sander
- Scraper
- Wood filler
- Putty knife
- Finishing materials of your choice

For Replacing Damaged Moldings
- Prybar for removing damaged sections
- Lengths of replacement molding
- Tape measure
- Contact cement
- Appropriate size finishing nails
- Miter box and backsaw
- Hammer

For Applying New Moldings
- Prybar for removing old moldings
- Lengths of new molding

- Tape measure and pencil
- Appropriate size finishing nails
- Miter box and backsaw
- Hammer and nailset
- Wood filler (for patching nail holes)
- Finishing materials of your choice

Repairing Damaged Moldings

You will need only to combine several skills covered elsewhere in this book.

Replacing Damaged Moldings

Replacing old moldings is something else. To return to that plank of solid 1" x 6" lumber that had been slapped up in our living room: exactly how might we go about matching this up with the old baseboard molding that lay undisturbed elsewhere in the room? Our naive answer was to take a spare scrap that we found lying around our basement to the lumber yard and ask them for a 4' replacement. Good chance. The salesperson had a nice long laugh on us. "You two must be new at this game, right?" The fact is that when he told us no place in the western hemisphere would stock replacements for the moldings we were showing

him, we naturally assumed that he was handing us the typical retailer's line: "If we don't have it, you won't find it anywhere." But four lumber-yards and two molding "specialty stores" later, we were ready to concede defeat.

Fortunately, you do have two practical solutions: Bring the scrap sample to a place that does millwork, where at a stiff price they will custom duplicate the design, or improvise your own replacement. We made the second choice and we still like to show off the proud results to first-time visitors to the house.

Shopping Suggestions

What it entails is visiting a lumber yard where they stock a variety of moldings and then picking out an assortment of individual designs which, when pieced together with glue, will *nearly* equal the original. Of course we can't give you instructions on how to do this for every kind of old molding (in fact your chances may be slim), but the general theory is easy to apply, so we'll illustrate the process using our own moldings as an example.

Here is a concise summary of how you can proceed, depending on the condition of your moldings when you start:

IF...	THEN...
1. Moldings are in reasonably good shape, though the paint is chipped here and there.	Scrape off any chipped paint, sand the bad spots smooth, wash down with all-purpose cleanser and a surface preparation, and then repaint.
2. Moldings are dented as well as chipped.	Wood fill the dents, molding the plastic wood to the shape of the trim, then proceed as above.
3. Detail in the moldings is *badly* obscured beneath many old coats of paint.	No choice here but to strip the paint or replace the moldings altogether. Still another new coat will be meaningless.
4. Moldings are damaged beyond repair.	Buy or improvise replacement moldings.

1.) Here's something close to what we wanted to replace:

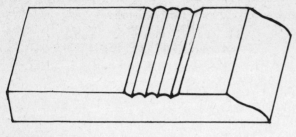

molding

2.) One available style we found called "one member base" looked like this:

molding

3.) We simply sawed off the lower section, leaving us with an approximation of (1), which was miraculously just about the precise thickness we needed.

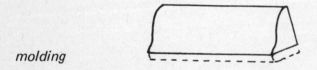

molding

4.) Next we ordered and cut down a thin rectangular strip equal to (2) (called "lattice" and used normally for building a trellis in a garden). This we had to back by double its own thickness to duplicate the original depth.

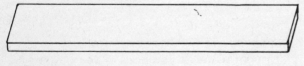

lattice strip

5.) Now we bought a length of what was called "shelf edge" molding to take care of section (3). This too needed to be backed with two thin lattice strips which we salvaged.

6.) That left section (4), a simple length of 1" x 4".

7.) To make all these separate lengths appear as if they were a single unit when we applied them to the walls, we simply performed a cut and paste operation which involved the use of small and large finishing nails, contact cement, and whatever other materials were necessary. The results were hardly distinguishable from the original design you saw back at (1). This is not, to be sure, the kind of procedure you'll find described in a classic text, but it certainly seemed to work for us.

Applying New Moldings

Sometimes, when the area you're working in has old trim that just isn't worth restoring, you may be best off using a prybar to remove it and buying new moldings altogether. Of course, you'd do the same in a room that had no moldings at all if you felt like adding them. Five steps are involved here:

1.) Measure the exact length of each strip you'll need throughout the room. Of course, you can use the old moldings as your guide if they were accurately cut. Bring these figures with you when you shop.

2.) Select a style that blends with the character of the room. You won't be able to match the old ones, but you may find something you like that's close. Where the walls meet the ceiling, you can choose from among cove, bed, crown, and many others. Where they meet the floors, baseboard molding is the thing to buy, and it is often nailed in combination with what is called *quarter round*. This *quarter* designation has nothing to do with quarters of an inch, as we first thought, but with the shape of the molding, which looks like a rod cut into quarters.

3.) Depending upon the current stock on hand in the lumber yard, you may find yourself buying long lengths and cutting them down. Occasionally, you may even wind up butting a strip or two. Let common sense guide you here.

4.) Once the wood is home, you're ready to measure out the individual pieces and saw them. This is where the process known as *mitering* comes in. When the molding is nailed to the wall, the strips will meet at right angles at the corners. Obviously, you don't want these to come together in an awkward overlap with only one side touching the corner. So you saw the ends at opposing 45° angles inside a miter box.

a.) Secure the miter box to your workbench so that it can't slide around when you saw.

b.) Measure the first length of wall to be covered. Transfer this measurement to the molding by making a pencil mark at the top of the strip near the *back* (the surface, that is, which will lie *against* the wall).

c.) Place the wood in the miter box *on its edge* (not lying flat, as you would for a window, door, or picture frame) and line up the pencil point with the appropriate slot—the one that will let you saw in the proper direction.

d.) Hold the molding with one hand to secure it well, and lower your backsaw over the wood so that its direction conforms with the angled grooves.

e.) Hold the saw level to the wood surface, and stroke gently to begin the cut.

f.) Increase your stroke and continue sawing until the wood is severed.

g.) As each new piece is cut, number it consecutively on the back in pencil so you don't confuse the order.

Complications that seem to plague almost every beginner:

a.) Make certain that your cut is angled in the right direction. You always have two possible ways to go, and one is always wrong. The choice depends on whether you're mitering for an outside or an inside corner, and of course on whether you're sawing the left or the right piece.

b.) Don't allow the saw to move off course. The box's guiding grooves are cut just wide enough to allow the blade to move back and forth freely. But it's important not to let the saw widen these grooves still further because then the accuracy of the angle will be destroyed. Once this happens, the notches are of no further use.

c.) Since the guiding grooves are cut only so deep into the sides of the miter box, you may need to prop up the board you're cutting by setting a thickness of scrap wood under it sometime during the sawing process.

d.) Your old house may well have rooms whose corners do not form perfect 90° angles either because, as in the case of our dining room area, the shape is pentagonal or something else unusual, or because the angles are simply off. When this happens, you'll have to buy a more expensive steel miter box, which can be set to cut wood at any desired angle.

6.) Nail the strips to the studs in the wall with the appropriate size finishing nails. Countersink the heads with your nailset.

7.) For a finished appearance, wood fill the nailholes, and then either stain or paint over them. You may also have to use some filler in the corners to cover mitering mistakes.

DECORATIVE BEAMS

Overview

1.) Plan and sketch out the placement of the beams.
2.) Buy the required lumber.
3.) Gather the necessary materials.
4.) Stain the wood.
5.) Secure the beams to the ceiling.

First Considerations

It's easy to forget that generations ago ceiling beams were not left visible for the purpose of adding a touch of rustic charm to a room's decor. Today, their purpose is almost always purely decorative so that they rarely serve a structural function anymore. We've used them twice in our house—once to add character to our "country kitchen," and again to complement the stucco ceiling we put up in our master bedroom.

Materials

- Tape measure and pencil
- Required lumber (or prefabricated beams)
- Appropriate size lag screws and washers (or other hardware)
- Nails
- Electric drill and necessary bits
- Ladder
- Stain and staining rag
- Speed handle
- Wood filler
- Hammer
- Chisel or plane (if you need to do notching)

Shopping Suggestions

You might think that putting up decorative beams would just involve buying the required lengths of lumber in the standard dimensions of your choice—either 2'' x 4''s, 3'' x 4''s, or whatever—applying stain, and then securing them to the ceiling. As usual in this age of instant everything, imitation beams are now becoming more and more widely available to make your decisions more complicated. These are often prefabricated wood or plastic, but their surfaces are factory treated to resemble the real thing—complete with knot holes and distress marks to simulate old wood. Their impressive bulk is deceptive, too, because invariably the insides are hollowed out to cut down on material costs. (They *are*, admittedly, much lighter to handle.) Frankly, we have mixed feelings about these artificial beams. Something phony about the construction and design seems always to give them away. On the positive side, if you find a style that doesn't look cheap, as we succeeded in doing for our kitchen, they have the advantage of being easier to handle and install. Some are mounted with adhesive according to instructions provided by the manufacturer; others, usually the ones made of wood, get hammered in with matching hardware.

Our preference, though, is for standard lumber such as pine, fir, hemlock, or cedar which you can buy and finish yourself. The choice of dimensions is up to you. We used two 15' lengths of 2" x 4" for a proportioned look in our bedroom, but 3" x 4"s, 4" x 4"s, or 4" x 6"s are equally good, depending upon the size of the room. Naturally, they become trickier to manipulate as they get larger, but two people shouldn't have too difficult a time.

Steps

1. Plan and Sketch Out the Position of the Beams

The number of beams you put up and their spacing too is a matter of personal taste, so you'll have to decide this matter for yourself. The recommended plan is to locate the beams directly under the ceiling joists to provide them with a solid base. We used only two both times we did this work. On each occasion we ran them from left to right *across* the room (seen from the point of view of someone standing at the door looking in) to intersect the ceiling molding at right angles. But you can also use beams of the same dimension around the entire perimeter of the room, or even run them in a crisscross pattern.

These last two plans necessitate notching the beams at the points of intersection, which just means cutting out a block of wood from each of the pieces to be joined. Make a sketch, on paper, of the pattern that suits you, and then measure

your distances *carefully* before you visit the lumberyard. That way you can cut everything to your precise specifications. In fact, measure twice to make doubly sure.

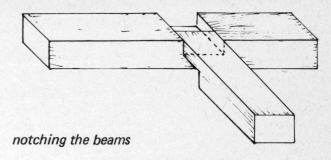

notching the beams

2. Mark Off the Correct Placement on the Ceiling

You are eventually going to secure the beams to the ceiling, which means that they will hold best when attached to the joists (wood beams which lie between the ceiling and the floor above). So the first step is locating those joists you plan to use. This is no different from finding the studs in a hollow wall. Once you've succeeded in hitting the first one, the remainder should be simple to find since each lies (you hope) 16" on center from the next. Decide where each decorative beam is to go, and mark its position according to your sketch with pencil and tape measure across the entire ceiling.

If you are putting up the hollowed-out beams we mentioned earlier, you can work things out so that the location of the joists need not be a limiting factor. 2" x 4"s (or whatever dimension of lumber can fit *inside* the hollow space) can be fastened to the ceiling with toggle bolts, and then the beams may easily be nailed to these whenever a joist is inconveniently located.

3. Stain the Wood In the Desired Color

It's better to stain the beams before you put them up so you don't spot the ceiling.

4. Secure the Beams to the Ceiling Joists

As soon as the stain dries, you're ready to attach the beams to the ceiling. You can use large finishing nails to do this, but there's a real danger of cracking the plaster as you hammer away, so we've found *lag screws* to be more practical. These are nothing more than long, heavy duty screws (up to 4" and more in length) with square or hexagonal heads that can be driven in with a special tool called a *speed handle*—a kind of socket wrench shaped much like a carpenter's hand brace. You will use as many screws as the length of the beam warrants, spacing them equidistantly. Put each one up with a washer to prevent the head from digging into the wood. Before you sink them, three different sized starter holes will have to be drilled. Hole #1 goes through the plaster and into the ceiling joists. It should correspond in diameter to the threads at the base of the lag screw, but this gets drilled through the decorative beam *only* and not into the joist. Hole #3 goes just deep enough into the decorative beam to allow you to countersink the head and washer. This may sound complicated, but the actual work goes quickly enough. Wood fill the holes after the beams are up, allow the putty to dry, and then stain it to match. Naturally if you have ceiling moldings in the room you'll have to saw away a section equal to the width of the beams at all points of intersection.

PANELING

Overview

1.) Measure the room.
2.) Select and purchase the required paneling.
3.) Gather the necessary materials.
4.) Organize the room for the job.
5.) Prepare the walls.
6.) If necessary, cut down the first panel to allow for a plumb installation.
7.) Nail the first piece.
8.) Butt and nail the remaining panels, sawing any cutouts as required.
9.) Add or restore trim.

First Considerations

The term *paneling* has become permanently associated in our minds with the walls in doctors' waiting rooms and fast food restaurants—those 4' x 8' sheets of processed sawdust with a wood veneer (or, worse still, a photograph of wood grain) glued to their surface. The choices available can easily overwhelm today's homeowner, including as they do such materials as cork, pegboard, formica, brick veneer, and even tin. We are obviously not crazy about this stuff, especially for older houses. One of our first remodeling ef-

forts, in fact, was to hide the paneled kitchen walls that the previous owners had installed as a modern improvement by covering them over with 7" widths of shiplapped pine—*real* wood which we merely stained lightly and left unfinished. We include directions for putting up sheet paneling, first of all because we realize that the prefinished panels have become indispensable for literally millions of people in this country, and secondly because we are willing to concede, snobs that we are, that the finer kinds of genuine plywood paneling can indeed be attractive.

As with sheetrocking, the project in this book which it most resembles, paneling with 4' x 8' sheets is easiest when your wall is flat and unobstructed by doors, windows, electrical outlets, and switches. Even with these intrusions, though, the job is no big deal, since a saber saw can quickly take care of any cutouts.

It's important to take these considerations into account before you measure the walls or buy your panels. That way you'll know from the start exactly what kind of installation job you'll have on your hands. The actual physical work (nailing furring strips or whatever else) can be done after you've brought the panels home and set the room up for the job.

Shopping Suggestions

When you visit the lumberyard or paneling supply store, bring with you an accurate set of measurements listing the dimensions of each wall to be paneled and include obstructions such as windows and doors. It's much better to give them the responsibility of calculating your needs. That way you can usually make returns on unused sheets. Don't resist if they urge you to buy one extra; you'll need it for piecing or rectifying mistakes. Do take the precaution, though, of asking that a notation be made on your sales slip allowing you to bring back any excess panels when the job is complete.

Since we are not paneling fans, we won't offer you detailed advice on what to buy. A few miscellaneous suggestions, though: Don't get less than 3/8" thickness. Stay away from the super-cheap patterns. If there is matching molding and/or nails for the particular style you've chosen, take home the amount you'll need. If you have higher than 8' ceilings, inform your dealer, and he'll show you a range of styles that come in 4' x 10.'

The most important variable is the wall you start out with. Here are the most common possibilities:

IF YOUR STARTING WALL IS . . .	YOU SHOULD . . .
1. Sheetrock nailed to studs, with or without wallpaper or paint.	Nail new paneling through the sheetrock and into the studs or attach it with a recommended adhesive.
2. Plaster, with or without wallpaper or paint, whose surfaces are level and smooth.	Nail new paneling through the plaster into the studs or install it with a recommended adhesive.
3. Uneven, regardless of surface material.	Nail 1" x 2" furring strips to the studs, 48" on center vertically and 16" horizontally. Use 8d (2½") common nails. Check the results with a level. Plane down or build up with thin shims of wood any sections that are not perfectly flat, and then nail the new paneling to these.
4. Masonry.	Attach furring strips as above, but with cut nails or nail anchors (no easy job!). Again, the surface must be completely level for good result.
5. Old paneling.	Nail right over it. Old panels provide extra insulation and an additional nailing base.

Materials

(The items you'll need will depend upon the type of installation job you're doing.)
- Panels sufficient for the job
- Hammer
- Proper size finishing nails
- Saber saw and fine tooth blade (or crosscut handsaw)
- Pencil
- Tape measure
- Wood filler in matching color
- Nailset
- Level and square
- Compass
- (Moldings)
- (Caulking gun and adhesive)
- Drill and bit

Steps

1. Organize the Room for the Job

Take out any furniture that can be removed easily, and detach from the walls any shelves or hanging units you intend to panel over. Pry off the ceiling and baseboard moldings. If they're in decent condition and blend well with the color of the paneling you plan to install, by all means save and renail them later since it will cut hours off the job if you can get away without having to cut and miter a whole new set of moldings. This is also the time to locate all the studs in the room. To make your work easy, mark their position clearly with a pencil on the ceilings and floor. If they are spaced properly, 16" on center, and if the walls, whether plaster or sheetrock, are solid and level, you should be off to a smooth start. Incidentally, a work table placed in the center of the room for sawing is a helpful added convenience.

2. Prepare the Walls

If you're not so lucky as to have studs that are evenly located, or if you're dealing with masonry walls or surfaces that are sloped or irregular, you'll have no choice but to install a sufficient quantity of 1″ x 2″ furring strips and construct a network of wood framing to which the panels can be nailed. Use the previous chart as your guide.

3. Prepare the First Sheet for Nailing

There are two matters to attend to before you put up the first panel. Once you've taken care of them, almost nothing can go wrong.

The placement of the studs is crucial. Since your panels are all 4′ wide (48″), you'll be properly set up for nailing if they lie exactly 16″ apart on center. Let's be optimistic for a moment and assume that they are. Let's also assume that you're wise enough to begin with a wall that isn't broken by windows or doors. The first panel will be placed in the left corner of the starting wall and nailed to the first four studs.

The one essential principle to observe is this. Always make sure that the panels are nailed so that the beginnings and ends of each meet directly over a stud. This means that in nailing the right side of Panel #1 to Stud D, you cannot overlap further than half the width of the stud, or you'll have nowhere to begin nailing Panel #2.

If the edges of the panels *don't* meet over a stud, there's no way you'll be able to keep the wall

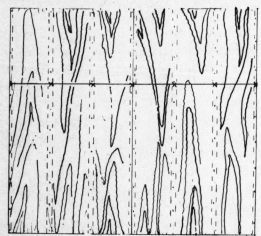

stud positioning

level. If (heaven spare you!) the studs are unequally spaced, you'll have to cut up and piece the panels *somehow* so that this rule is *always* observed.

The other factor is the starting corner. By now you should be prepared to discover that it is less than perfectly plumb. That will mean cutting off a portion of the left side of the panel so that the *right* side can lie absolutely vertical. Once this has been done, each subsequent panel will, of necessity, be vertical too.

a.) Take a tape measure and, standing on a ladder, mark a pencil point 50″ to the right of the starting corner along the ceiling line. That's exactly 2″ longer than the width of the panel.

b.) Tap a nail into the pencil mark temporarily, and attach to it a plumb line whose surface has been well coated with colored chalk.

c.) With the weight holding the line taut, snap the string. The chalk mark that results should be perfectly plumb.

d.) Remove the plumb line and nail. Rest the first panel against the wall so that its right side conforms exactly to the chalk line. Have someone hold it in place while you proceed.

e.) Now take an ordinary compass, and open it to a precise 2″ spread. With the metal tip held in the left corner of the wall and the pencil tip held against the edge of the panel, move the compass along the entire vertical distance between ceiling and floor. Don't allow the angle of the compass to shift while you do this. You'll notice that the pencil will now automatically mark the panel for cutting.

f.) Carry the panel to your workbench, and position it so that the finished side lies face down. Now cut along the penciled guideline with either a crosscut saw or a saber saw fitted with a fine tooth blade.

4. Install the First Sheet

"Install" can mean nail or glue, but we have had some unfortunate experiences with adhesives, so our preference is for nailing. You may be persuaded otherwise.

Carry the panel back to its position against the wall, this time bringing its left edge flush with the corner. It's a good idea to have someone help you to hold it ¼″ or so above the floor while you nail—you'll need the extra space if the wood expands with time. If this proves awkward or difficult, use

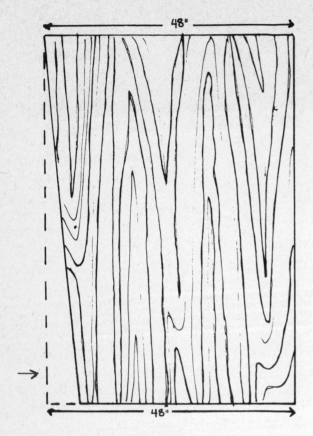
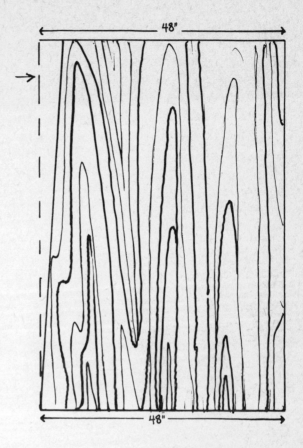

guidelines for cutting panels

wood shims between floor and panel. All things being equal, you should use 8d finishing nails (2½''). Hammer them into the ''V'' grooves that divide the strips which make up each sheet of paneling. Begin nailing at the center and work out to the sides. Remember that the right vertical edge of the sheet *must* be nailed to the *center* of a stud so that the next sheet can meet it over a nailing surface. Drive in the nails so that they're almost flush; you don't want to mar the wood surface with the hammer. Later on, when all the sheets are up, you will countersink them with a nailset and wood fill the holes with a matching color plastic wood.

5. Butt and Nail the Remaining Panels, Sawing the Cutouts as Required

Everything is easier from here on in. Since each subsequent panel must be butted perfectly to the one installed before it, the position of each is predetermined. The only thing that can hold you up is an irregularity in the spacing of the studs, but we hope you've already tended to this. Cutouts for doors, windows, or electrical boxes should pose no special problems. Just be very patient with your measurements. They must be transferred with a pencil to the backs of the panels with perfect accuracy before you begin cutting. For internal cuts with the saber saw, drill a hold someplace *inside* the cutout area, lower the blade into position, and move it along your guidelines. The very last piece of paneling will no doubt have to be measured and cut specially to fit.

6. Add the Trim

Adding moldings not only gives the room a finished look; it allows you to conceal any minor unevenness along the floor.or ceiling lines. More important, you can use what's called corner guard to nail over both the inside and outside corners— especially handy if you've done some sloppy measuring. Many prefinished panels today are sold with moldings to match, but you can buy natural wood trim and stain and finish it to your taste. All the directions you'll need for selecting, mitering, and nailing can be found in the moldings section earlier in this chapter.

Chapter 10

Ceramic Tiling

Overview

1.) Measure the room to decide how much tile you need.
2.) Purchase the required tile.
3.) Gather the necessary materials.
4.) Remove all existing tile where necessary.
5.) Prepare the walls and/or floors for tiling.
6.) Cut and apply the tile.
7.) Apply the grout.

First Considerations

Although more people warned us against doing our own tiling than any other project, we also noticed that all the tile stores sold do-it-yourself equipment and seemed to have an active clientele. We debated the pros and cons, eventually deciding to buy the materials and give it a try. If the job became too much for us, we could always call an "expert." As things turned out, we *did* accomplish what we had set out to do, successfully mounting ceramic tile on walls and floors, despite much trial and error and little help from published sources.

Your work, complicated enough as it is, can be made slightly more or less so, depending upon the already existing surfaces.

• Is there unwanted ceramic tile up already?
• Is there some other material covering the surface (like vinyl tile on the floor)?
• Must you remove it?
• In what condition is the wall or floor below?
• Will it be damaged by the removal of what is presently covering it?

Your room may already be tiled, but you may not like the color. A petty reason to give for going to much trouble and expense? Not necessarily. But color is only one small reason for ripping out

tile. In an old house, the tile may be cracked in some spots and discolored in others. Finally, as in our case, it may have been put on poorly and thus, combined with its color, present an eyesore.

Books sometimes say that you can place new ceramic tile over already existing tile. We doubted the advisability of such a step for the walls, primarily because the second layer of tile would protrude too far, and the edges which can be seen from the side would be unsightly. Nor could the new floor be effectively applied atop the old one because the present vinyl was neither smooth nor even.

Consequently, we removed all existing tile; that was the easy part. The first surprise came when we realized what we were left with, aside from cartons of broken tile. The walls enclosing the tub were made of sheetrock, the top layer of which was now in the garbage still attached to the back of the old white and gold marbelized tile fragments. After some brief agonizing, we decided to look on the bright side: this would force us to learn how to put up a new wall. The second surprise hit us when we pulled up a few squares of vinyl floor tile. We found several kinds of floors—part warped wood, part cracked cement, part undiscernible altogether. The Pollyanna in us immediately rose to the challenge, and we learned to level the floor and cut plywood to make a new subfloor. We concluded that whenever you rip out old tile, you will probably have to replace or refinish the surface below.

Shopping Suggestions

A quick look through the yellow pages or a ride along any commercial highway should reveal any number of tile stores. Their merchandise may range from common 4¼" x 4¼" pastel bathroom tiles selling for approximately ninety cents per square foot to hand-painted ceramic imports for up to $14.00 per square foot!

No guarantees can be made, but, in general, the salespeople are quite willing to assist you; few customers can operate without their help. They do not expect you to know how much tile you need, but they will ask you what size area you want to cover. The smart thing to do is to make a diagram of your room. If walls are to be included, as well as the floor, indicate on the side of your diagram the height from the floor to the point where you want your tile to stop.

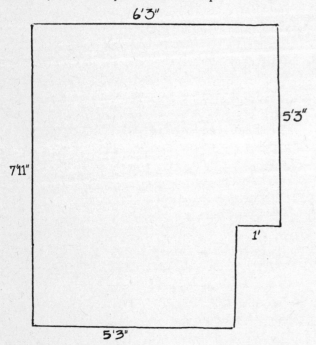

floor plan of bathroom

If you carry your floor plan in your wallet, you will have it to show to the salesperson, and he will be able to convert your dimensions into the tile requirements.

Read *all* the little signs above the store counter, even if they are small and seem unimportant. Usually the signs announce one of three things: a penalty of from 10-50% on all returned merchandise, a time limit on all returns, and a no-return policy on certain tile. All these notices seem to contradict the breezy manner of the salesperson who tells you to buy extra tile because "You can always return it!"

You do have to buy a little extra tile because

you will always break some with the tile cutter, but if your style selection is a relatively common one, and you live fairly near the store, you can always make additional trips.

We dealt with two stores and in each case had trouble with returns. It was with great effort that we finally found the tiles we wanted for our walls, but the order arrived just as we were leaving on vacation. There was only a two week return period, but they assured us that there would be no problem. We probably should have asked them to put the promise in writing, but looking back now, we're sure they would have refused, saying it was unnecessary . . . "Trust us."

When our vacation was over and the tiling done, we went to return the extras, but the owner's daughter, who had written up the original sale, almost refused to take the return since a month had elapsed; when we were firm she admitted to being sorry that she had made any promises but reluctantly accepted our leftover tile, deducting the posted "return penalty." If you are confused by the "return penalty policy," you are not alone. There is no logic to it; you can return an unworn garment with no questions asked, but you cannot return unused and untouched tile without losing money in the transaction.

The floor tile conflict had an even unhappier ending. We gave the proprietor of the second store a floor plan of our room, and as he estimated our needs, we could have sworn (and to this day still do) that he gave us the "Don't worry . . . you can always return what you don't use" routine. When we did, indeed, return with almost twenty dollars worth of unused tile, he pointed to a very small sign to the right above the main counter, not directly in front of the main counter itself where a customer was most likely to see it. The sign read "NO RETURNS ON FLOOR TILE." If you are trying to find a logic in such a policy, once again let us warn you not to waste your valuable time. One can only conclude that in the free enterprise system, a man can set down whatever regulations he wishes as long as he runs the show. No amount of crying, pleading, or screaming got us past his arrogance or won us our money back. We now check all walls for signs and read all small print before we sign!

A word about the kind of tile to select. Your choice may be affected by style of decorating, practicality, and cost.

If you seek a modern impression, you might look to the glazed quarry tiles for your floor. They are rather costly, but they are easy to care for and are very attractive to look at. Also, most bathrooms have less floor space than other areas of the house which lend themselves to tile, so this might be a good area in which to splurge.

If you want a more traditional look, or are working on a small budget, you would probably turn to the unglazed tiles for the floor—the common tile found in most homes and public restrooms. We chose these since we could find them in the old hexagonal shape. Whether it be the white color or the dull surface, unfortunately they are hard to care for. They don't clean well and show dirt easily. We still like the look, but we must admit that they are something of a disappointment.

Before we put down the ceramic tile, the floor was covered with vinyl squares. Of course these or linoleum are always usable, but somehow we associate them with kitchens or playrooms; this is purely a matter of taste. The most common tile for walls are the 4¼" x 4¼" glazed tiles which come in the standard pastel colors. Mosaic tile can be used for walls, floors, or counter tops.

In summary, then, try to develop a decorating concept for the room as a whole. Study your finances to determine approximately how much you want to spend. With these two things in mind, go to the stores and see what will best satisfy your needs.

Materials

For Removing Old Tile
- Putty knife
- Large screwdriver or cold chisel
- Hammer
- Several cartons (strong cardboard)

For Preparing Walls For Tiling
If you must replace the plasterboard
- Sheets of 4' x 8' plasterboard (waterproof, if possible)
- Spackle knife
- Electric sander with sandpaper (medium and fine grade)
- Crowbar
- Sheetrock nails (also called blue nails, for use specifically with plasterboard)
- Hammer

- Pencil
- Paper tape for plasterboard (to smooth the crack between butted sheets of plasterboard)
- Jigsaw
- Tape measure (or yardstick)
- Spackle

If you must repair a plaster wall
- Electric sander with sandpaper (coarse and medium grade)
- Spackle
- Spackle knife

For Leveling the Floor
- Level
- Odd pieces of plywood and cardboard
- Flash Patch (if needed)
- Putty knife
- Pail
- Assorted nails
- Scissors
- Tape measure (or yard stick)
- Jigsaw
- Pencil

For Making a New Underfloor
- ½" exterior plywood
- 8d nails
- Large sheets of brown wrapping paper
- Pencil
- Tape measure (or yard stick)
- Scissors
- Scotch tape (or narrow masking tape)
- Jigsaw

For Mounting Tiles on Walls or Floors
- Adhesives (Floor and wall use different adhesives)
- Cardboard
- Grout (for walls) or joint compound (for floors)
- Bucket to mix grout or joint compound
- Several sponges
- Several abrasive cloths (towels, burlap)
- Turpentine
- Felt pen, pencil, ruler
- Tile cleaner
- Grout sealer
- Sheets of plastic (for floor tiling only—enough to cover floor)

- Pliers
- Coarse sandpaper
- To rent: Tile cutter (rented by the day from tile store)

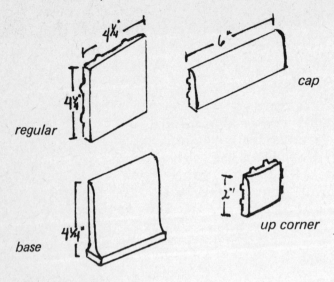

regular

cap

base

up corner

shapes of tiles

Steps

1. Remove All Existing Tile Where Necessary

Some of you will be able to skip this section. If, for example, you choose to take a wall that was previously covered only by paint, you may be able to go on to Step 2. If, like us, you must remove the old tile, read on.

The task of removing tile is not so much difficult as it is messy. Keep a carton next to you as you take a tool with a thin edge, like a screwdriver, cold chisel, or putty knife, and dig it into the most vulnerable edge of the tile—a slightly loose or cracked piece or a section where the grout between the tiles is weak—pulling away from the surface towards you. Once you have one tile or a portion of tile off, you have opened a path to the rest; just keep digging under and prying off pieces, filling your cartons as you go.

When all the tiles have been removed, what remains is not likely to be a very pretty sight. The big question really is: can I make the wall smooth enough for a new tile surface, or will I have to replace the wall?

2. Prepare the Surface for Tiling

If your old ceramic tile was glued to sheetrock, there is a good chance that part of the top layer was ripped off as you tore away the tile. There is almost no way that this can be avoided; you can't just try to be careful. If the glue adheres to the sheetrock, they will come off together. Also, even if the sheetrock remains intact, it will be covered with uneven dried globs of adhesive. How will you remove it? The top layers of sheetrock are paper and cannot take to heavy sanding, scraping, or application of chemicals.

With a combination of hammer and crowbar, you'll have to hack out the old wall—sheetrock is not very hard and is at most ½" thick—trying to get large pieces that can be carried directly out of the room. If you get small pieces, put them in the boxes with the old tile. Once you make a hole in the wall, you will see how easily the rest of the wall comes down.

If the wall beneath the old tile is plaster, you may be able to save it. With an electric sander, sand off whatever old tile adhesive remains on the wall, first using the coarse grade of sandpaper. Then patch up any holes in the plaster with spackle.

If the plaster wall is ruined, then you will have to hack it out just as you would with a plasterboard one and replace it with a new sheetrock wall.

If the wall is smooth but covered with paint, sand the wall with coarse sandpaper just to remove the shiny surface that might prevent the tiles from sticking.

Finally, if the wall has wallpaper on it, you can leave the wallpaper up as long as it is on firmly. If it is on loose, you must remove it in order to have a solid surface on which to rest the tiles.

3. Install the Tiles

On the day you plan to start the actual tiling (or better still, late the afternoon before), go to your nearest ceramic tile store and rent a tile cutter. Most of the tiles, fortunately, will not have to be cut. Rarely, however, will you get to the end of the row and find the last tile fitting perfectly. That's when the tile cutter comes in. Have the salesperson demonstrate the machine, and then ask to try it yourself. Also make sure that the little rotating blade is sharp or your job will be that much more difficult.

When you have all your tools and supplies assembled, you can get down to work.

Your first job is measuring. The height of the

tile can vary in different areas of the room, but a good rule to follow is to plan to lay the top row of tile at least one row above the shower head in the tub area (you can do it all the way to the ceiling if you wish) and two rows above the toilet and sink.

The professional sources do not always agree on where to begin the tiling—at the top or at the bottom. We decided to start at the top for reasons that we'll explain shortly.

Before You Start the Application

a.) If you are not tiling all the way to the ceiling, place a yardstick at one end of the first wall to be tiled, and measure from the ceiling down to the point where you want your top row of tile to rest. Put a pencil mark at this point.

b.) Take a similar measurement approximately every two feet, and connect the resulting pencil marks. You should now have a horizontal line parallel to the ceiling.

c.) Follow the above steps for each wall being tiled regardless of the height of the top row of tile.

unsightly errors at eye level if you work quickly. Yes, we used appearance—how things looked to the eye—as our guide. We knew that the bottom of most rows would be obscured, in the case of the tub, by the shower curtain and, in other areas, by the fixtures and other decorative items. Thus we felt that it would please the eye to see the ceiling line and the tile line running parallel.

How to Apply the Tiles

Although the adhesive cans usually give good instructions, you can profit also from our experience. Work one small area at a time, starting in a corner at the height you have chosen.

a.) Apply a quantitiy of adhesive to the wall with your trowel, spreading it evenly over approximately one square foot at a time. The can says it takes a few hours to dry, but within fifteen minutes it becomes fairly difficult to work with.

b.) Take two cap tiles and place them with their upper surfaces resting on the pencil line. (If

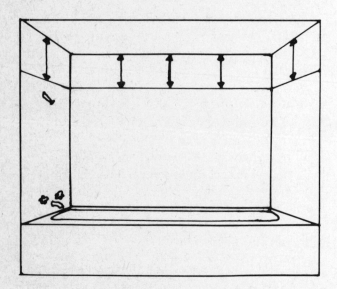

horizontal guideline

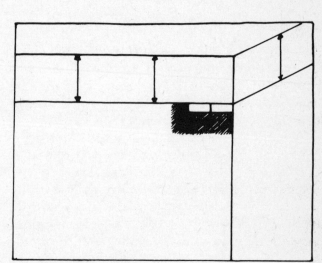

starting cap tiles

d.) Wherever necessary, remove all accessories such as towel bars, curtain rods, light plates, handles from faucets, and moldings.

e.) Always start in a corner, using whole tiles if possible.

f.) Start tiling at the top along your pencil line. Although this rule defies gravity, and the tiles might slide a bit at first, this method avoids

you are starting at the ceiling, you will not need caps. Start directly with your regular tiles.)

c.) Below them, cover the rest of the glued area with your regular tiles, working in neat rows and butting the top of one tile into the bottom of the one below it. The tiles are constructed so as to allow room for the grout to fit in naturally as the tile surfaces hit each other.

d.) Working downward, spread adhesive over the next square foot, and line up the next few rows of tile. Check for tile slippage and push up any that have started to slide down.

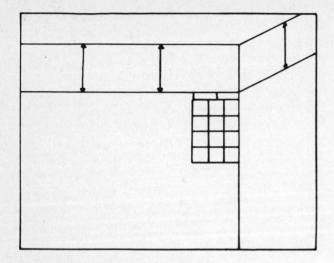

starting rows of 4¼" x 4¼" tiles

e.) Continue the same procedure until you get close to the bottom. Here is where the tile cutter may be needed for the first time—when a whole tile cannot fit. If you do not have floor molding or do not intend to put any on, you will be placing a row of base tiles in at the very bottom. Since, for the sake of appearance, you want to keep these tiles whole, you may have to cut the row of tiles above it to make the bottom row fit. Thus, put in the base tiles first, and then go back and measure the last row of regular tiles to fit the remaining

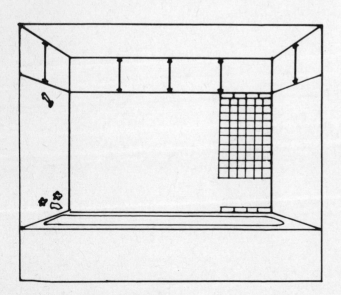

almost completed section

space. If you do have molding, cut the last row of tiles to meet the floor. (If you did not remove the molding, cut the tiles to meet the molding.)

f.) Now you can go back up to the top, starting with two more cap tiles and working your way down.

g.) If you plan to end the tile before a corner or at an outside corner, the edge will be in full view. Thus, allow enough room for a vertical row of cap tiles, headed by a small tile called an up corner tile. This last vertical row of caps gives a smooth finish to a wall that does not extend into a corner.

Even the most careful worker is going to get some adhesive on the front of the tiles. Don't panic. Put some turpentine or benzine on a rag and rub gently over the affected area.

On Tile Cutting

In some sense, tile cutting is an art. As you will see when you try it, a perfect technique takes time to develop.

a.) When you come to a place where a whole tile won't fit, measure your remaining space, take a tile, and mark off that same measurement on both sides of the front surface.

b.) Connect the two marks with a line, using a pencil or felt pen whose ink can be erased, and a ruler.

c.) Place the marked tile in the cutter, and line up the blade with your markings.

d.) Draw the cutting blade across the tile, as you were shown in the store, in one quick move.

e.) Finally, press down on the hand clamp, and the tile should be smoothly broken in two at exactly the right spot.

The tile cutter makes straight cuts only. If you must cut a tile to fit around a hole or a curve (e.g., around the faucet opening in the tub area), you must chip away at the tile a bit at a time with the pliers and smooth it out with coarse sandpaper. Most such cutouts will be covered by hardware (the faucet opening by the handle) or filled in with grout (the base of the toilet).

4. Apply the Grout

Grout is a plasterlike substance that is used to fill in spaces between the tiles. Grouting, or the applying of the compound, is not as difficult a task as it might seem. Do wait twenty four hours, though, after the tiles are in place to begin the grouting.

Instructions on the grout itself are self-explanatory for the most part. Follow them, keeping in mind the following:

a.) Whatever kind of grout you use, once it is ready to apply, dip your sponge into the grout and work it into the joints between each tile. Of course, you will get grout on the tile surfaces too, but this will be removed in the next step.

b.) Use rubber gloves if you can work comfortably with them.

c.) Have several sponges on hand to apply grout; have another set of sponges for removing excess grout from tile surfaces. Try to rinse them out as often as possible to keep grout from hardening in the pores.

d.) Have a clean water supply handy at all times, preferably a sink with water running.

e.) When removing excess grout from the joints after it has set for a few minutes, you may wonder how much to remove. Try to picture what most tiled bathroom walls look like. The grout never rises above the surface of the tile, but it does cover the spaces completely. Above all, be consistent in your touch. Don't make the joints thin in one spot and thick in another.

f.) It is not easy to remove the film left by the grout, so replace your rags often; the dirtier the rag, the harder it is to clean the wall.

FLOORS

1. Remove All Existing Tile Where Necessary

Most bathrooms have some kind of tile on the floor already because it is obviously most practical in a place where water is likely to fall or drip on it. If you don't have tile there already, and the existing floor is smooth and level, you can proceed directly to Step 3. If any of these conditions do not exist, read on.

Preparing a floor usually involves removing old tile when necessary and making sure the floor is level. Old tile must be removed and/or a new sub-floor put down if the existing floor is not smooth or secure enough to allow new tiles to be glued on top of it. In that case, pry them off with a putty knife, and hope that the floor below is better.

2. Prepare the Surface for Tiling

It is not likely that the floor you find underneath will be uniformly level and smooth, and you may have to make it level and put down a new plywood sub-floor over it.

To Level the Sub-floor

By placing a level at different spots on the bare floor, you can determine whether or not your floor is level. If it is not, ten new sub-floors above

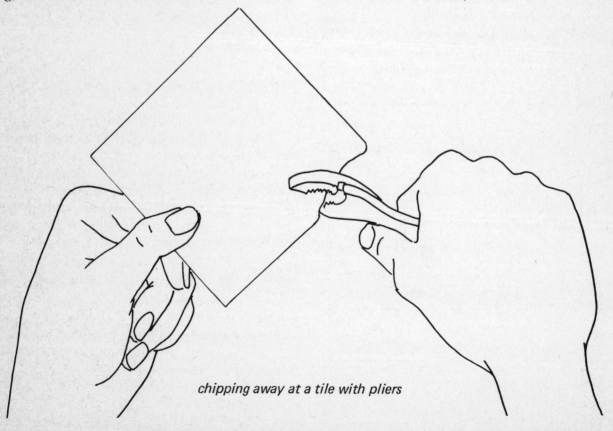

chipping away at a tile with pliers

it will not help you. You must make the old floor level first.

There are several things you can use to level a floor, depending upon how serious the slope is. Usually you will end up using several things, including Flash Patch, scraps of plywood, and pieces of cardboard. They will all help to build up areas that are lower than the rest of the floor. Basically, it's a matter of trial and error; see what fits in best in each spot. Flash Patch is a substance that comes in powder form and, when mixed with water, functions as concrete would. If below your old tile is a cracked concrete floor, this product can help you to fix it. Follow directions on the package for more specific information. Pieces of plywood can be nailed in where possible or secured with the tile adhesive, which is what you would use to keep the cardboard or corrugated paper in place.

Cutting and Securing the Plywood

It would be a simple procedure indeed to cut a plywood sub-floor for a bathroom that has no fixtures in it, and certainly if you plan to replace a sink, toilet, or tub in addition to putting down a new floor, first rip out the old fixtures, but don't replace them until you lay the new floor. Some books on tiling give instructions for removing toilet bowls and sinks, but we were not about to try that. We were sure that we would never be able to put them back!

In order to get a stiff 4' x 8' sheet of plywood to fit on a floor that is broken up by all sorts of obstructions, prepare a pattern as follows:

a.) Lay brown paper on one section of the floor at a time.

b.) With a pencil, trace around poles, pipes, toilet, sink bases, etc. in that area, making scissor cuts where necessary to mold the paper.

c.) With a scissors, cut along your pencil lines, and try fitting your pattern into the area it was designed to cover.

If you have not cut away enough, trim a bit more; if you have taken away too much, try to patch up your mistakes with small bits of brown paper and tape. Then check one more thing. When the piece is transformed from flexible paper to inflexible plywood, will it still be able to slide into the appropriate spot? If the answer is no, you may have to cut the pattern into smaller pieces.

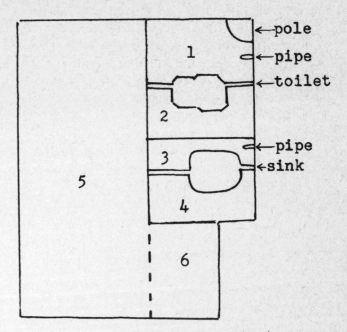

pattern to use for cutting plywood subfloor

When you are satisfied with your first pattern piece, go to your workbench.

a.) Place the paper on top of the plywood at one corner, and secure the pattern with a few pieces of tape.

b.) Trace it with a pencil and then remove the pattern piece.

c.) Cut along the pencil lines with your jigsaw.

d.) Bring the newly cut piece into the bathroom and try to fit it into place. If it is still too large, note the problem with a pencil, and trim the wood again with the jigsaw.

As you go on to the next pattern piece, allow a ¼" gap between pieces; they should not rest directly next to one another. Do the difficult pieces first, saving the large ones with no obstructions for last. When all pieces of wood are cut and in place, nail them down securely, using an 8d nail every few inches.

3. Install the Tiles

If you have already done wall tiling, floor tiling will hold few surprises. Although there are differences, you will no longer be intimidated by the thick adhesives or the moody tile cutting machines. Just make sure that you have bought ceramic floor tile adhesive. You cannot use the same kind that you used on the walls.

If the tiles you use are small, you may find that they come arranged on sheets backed by a kind of paper mesh or by gauze. This simplifies your task because you can work in larger sections in a shorter space of time. If you are using large tiles, they will come individually as do most wall tiles. In either case, most of the tiles can be placed in a manner similar to the wall tiles, basically following the directions on the adhesive can.

a.) Before you lay any adhesive, try out several sheets of tile (or individual tiles) in a row across the room, starting in one corner. See how many you can use uncut, and mark off the ones that need cutting. Cut them, and when that row is ready, pull the tiles away and apply the adhesive.

b.) Apply adhesive to a section of the floor with your trowel, covering at least enough for a sheet of tile and then, as you gain experience, for a row. Use pressure as you spread the adhesive smoothly.

c.) Set down a sheet of tile (or individual tiles) immediately, pressing the tiles in firmly. Since the mesh is flexible, make sure the rows are even and properly spaced.

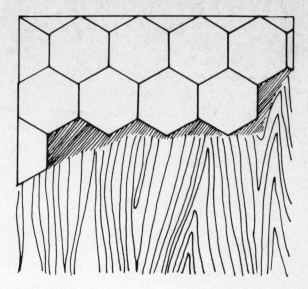

same section of floor with cut tiles filling in spaces

e.) Repeat this process for the remainder of the floor.

f.) As you work, you may find that a tile seems loose. Don't be afraid to pick it up and reglue it.

g.) If you get adhesive on the surface of the tile, rub gently with a rag soaked in turpentine.

4. Apply the Joint Filler

For a floor, we were advised to use joint filler instead of grout. Joint filler serves the same function, but because it is a stronger and more wear-resistant substance, it is better suited for use on a floor.

As with the walls, proceed according to the directions on the bag. These additional instructions may also prove helpful:

a.) Use rubber gloves if you can work with them comfortably.

b.) Make sure all spaces are well filled and tightly packed with the joint filler. As with the wall tile, have lots of sponges and rags to facilitate the cleaning process.

c.) Note any differences in the use of joint filler and grout; for example, the directions on the brand we used calls for dusting the surfaces with dry joint filler as soon as the wet filler firms up in the joints.

d.) When the joint filler is dry, any remaining film on the tiles can be removed by rubbing with wet cloths that have an abrasive quality (e.g., burlap or terry cloth).

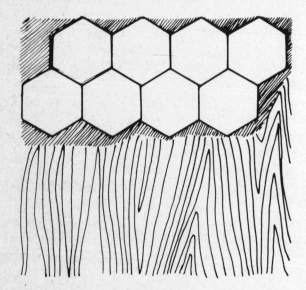

initial placing of floor tiles

d.) Continue this same application of adhesive followed by placement of tiles until you come to the spots where the whole sheet or tile cannot fit. Insert the tiles you have just cut for those places.

Chapter 11

Insulation

Overview

1.) Check your house, room by room, for drafts, cold spots, and open spaces that should be sealed.
2.) Measure the size of each area that needs insulating.
3.) Acquaint yourself with the possible materials available for each job.
4.) Shop for the necessary materials.
5.) Caulk and/or weatherstrip doors, moldings, outlets, and windows, where needed.
6.) Insulate accessible floors, ceilings, and walls with fiberglass blanket insulation if enough is not already there.
7.) Install storm windows, dampers, and other heat-saving devices, where possible.

First Considerations

Insulation is a very fashionable subject today. The energy crisis which has made its effects known in so many ways is no doubt responsible for this surge of interest in what was once a rarely talked about aspect of home maintenance. But saving heat and, consequently, money are not the only reasons for weatherproofing; a cold, drafty house is no fun live and entertain in. And because none of the materials are very difficult to install, you should not be intimidated by the job. With the United States government promising you that any money spent on insulation will be made up in less than one heating season, followed by year after year of clear saving, it does seem tempting to investigate.

How do you decide where to insulate and what to use? A careful tour of your home from top to bottom should reveal very plainly where the need for weatherproofing lies. Wherever you feel a draft, be it a whisper of air between the base-

board and the floor or a gust at the doorway to the attic, caulking and weatherstripping must be done. Whenever a room feels cold, even though the heat is up, insulation in the form of fiberglass blankets or blown-in wool or foam should be added to the floor, ceiling, and walls. The fiberglass blanket, most commonly sold in a roll, is the kind of insulation most often put in by homeowners themselves. It can be installed in the attic walls, floors, and ceilings or in any room where you have not yet put in the sheetrock or flooring. But what about the totally completed room which is in need of insulation? Recent years have seen the advent of a loose insulation that is neatly blown in. Most sources are in agreement, however, that this is not a do-it-yourselfer project, primarily because it involves special professional equipment. So, depending on the state of the room involved, you may have to work in combination with a contractor if your goal is a cozy, energy-saving home.

Further protective measures include: making sure that every window and door has a well-fitted storm, having a damper in every fireplace, and even considering the addition of wood paneling and outdoor siding for an extra layer of protection.

Shopping Suggestions

While you are making that tour of your house to check for drafts and cold spots, carry a pad, pencil, and tape measure. Whenever you come upon a vulnerable spot, jot down a brief description accompanied by its dimensions (below attic door—30''). When your list is complete, it will help you to determine how much and what kind of material you will need.

Caulking and weatherstripping are available in any store that sells hardware. Rolls of fiberglass blanket insulation are commonly found at lumberyards or home improvement stores. In any of these places, discuss your plans with the salesperson and see if you can get some free advice along with your purchase. So that you don't go into the store sounding completely uninformed, the following chart should give you an overview of the insulating scene:

Type of Insulation	Most Popular Products Available	How To Apply Them	Where To Use Them
weather stripping	felt weather stripping; comes in rolls; sold in various widths	staples or carpet tacks	doors, windows
	flexible vinyl gasket weather stripping; comes in rolls or strips; various widths	self-adhesive, or with tacks, staples, or glue	doors, windows
	rigid metal weather stripping, brass, bronze, or aluminum; sold in kits or by length	nails	doors, windows
	foam strips; comes in various widths	self-adhesive	doors, windows
	door bottoms/sweep strips; metal with plastic or felt; sold in kits	kits have appropriate nails or screws	doors
	transparent weather stripping tape; comes in rolls in various widths	self-adhesive	windows or wherever there is a crack
caulking	latex, silicone, butyl rubber, oil base or polyvinyl acetate	from a cartridge in a caulking gun	windows, door trim, moldings, electrical outlets
	caulking cord	in rope form, just press into place	windows
Fiberglass insulation	batts; rectangular blocks, faced in aluminum foil or kraft paper	staple	crawl spaces, small areas
	blankets; rolls, faced in aluminum foil or kraft paper	stapel	ceilings, walls, floors

Since no one will be able to use all the products on the chart, some recommendations may be in order. So far, we have used the sweep strips at the bottom of each door, the felt weatherstripping around the doors, and the transparent tape in several spots outdoors. Some people find the metal strips more efficient and longer lasting than the felt. This is probably true, but the felt is very inexpensive and easy to apply. For windows and moldings, we have found caulking either in the regular cartridge or cord form sufficient, especially since the installation of new, tight-fitting aluminum storms and screens. With the cartridges, latex caulking seems to be most popular because it takes paint more readily than other kinds and cleans up easily with plain water.

Fiberglass blanket insulation is more popular than the individual batts, but, in either case, the aluminum foil-faced varieties are recommended. The foil forms the best vapor barrier, keeping water vapor from penetrating the walls and condensing inside them. Since many brands of fiberglass insulation are on the market, just check to see how high its heat resistance rating is. The technical term for this quality is "R value." The higher the R value, the better job it does of insulating. Most sources agree that the insulation you buy for the ceiling should have an R value of 19 (approximately 6") and insulation for the walls and floors should have an R-11 value (approximately 3½" thick).

Materials

For Applying Weatherstriping
- Sufficient weatherstripping, any type and width
- Tape measure
- Ladder
- Scissors
- Tacks, nails, screws, staples and staple gun

For Applying Caulking
- Caulking of your choice in a cartridge and/or caulking cord
- Caulking gun
- Utility knife or scissors
- Putty knife
- Mineral spirits or water (depending on type of caulking)
- Rag

For Applying Fiberglass Blankets
- Sufficient aluminum foil-faced fiberglass blanket insulation
- Staple gun
- Staples (at least 5/16" long)
- Yardstick or plank of wood
- Felt-tipped pen
- Heavy work gloves
- Large shears or utility knife
- Contact cement or plastic tape

Steps: Weatherstripping

We have used the standard weatherstripping products primarily for doors, finding them less suitable for windows even though the packages show them on both. The felt and foam look un-

sightly, the tape is likely to take the paint with it when you remove it in the spring, and the metal can be complicated to attach. When I asked our hardware dealer what weatherstripping most people use on windows, he told us that they don't; they get good storm windows, and use caulking products to make them airtight.

After examining your own situation, and you choose to use a form other than the ones we discuss, just follow the illustrated directions on the package; they are usually easy to follow.

1. Apply Felt Weatherstripping to the Door Jamb
a.) Load your staple gun or gather your tacks and hammer.

b.) Position your ladder (if necessary) at the door.

c.) Take the roll of weatherstripping and, starting at the top of either side, staple or tack the felt onto the door jamb. When it is in position, the weatherstripping should make slight contact with the door when closed.

stapling weather stripping into door jam

The same process can be applied to the foam rubber weatherstripping, but since it is usually self-adhesive, you won't need tacks or staples.

2. Apply a Door Bottom (Sweep Strip) to the Lower Edge of the Door

a.) If the strip is larger than the width of your door, mark off the exact measurement, and remove the excess with a hack saw or a saber saw equipped with a fine tooth blade for cutting metal.

b.) Position the strip at the bottom of the door so the flexible part (plastic or felt) hangs below the door to block out the cold air.

c.) Fasten it to the wood with the nails or screws provided, placing one at each end and then working toward the center.

3. Cover any Other Cracks with Transparent Weatherstripping Tape, Unless You Plan to Use Caulking

Weatherstripping tape is transparent, but since it is still visible to the eye you will probably want to limit its use to areas not in full view (a hidden corner or an outer door that is closed permanently for the season). It comes in a roll and you can cut and apply pieces of any size, like you would any other tape.

Steps: Caulking

If you have ever worked with glazier's putty or even with spackle, caulking should not be a totally foreign substance. Because you can buy caulking in cartridges and apply it with a gun, it is easier to direct than the other substances once you become familiar with operating the tool.

Most homes have been caulked, at least around the windows, by either a former owner or the builder. You will have to do your own caulking when what is there is no longer functional, and air is coming through, or when you have found places which have never been filled at all. Caulking works very well along moldings and around electrical outlets, in addition to its standard use with windows.

a.) Remove old caulking, if it is cracked, by digging it out with a putty knife.

b.) Cut nozzle of caulking cartridge at a 45° angle with your utility knife or scissors. The lower down you make the cut, the wider the strip of caulking you will get.

c.) Fit the cartridge into the gun.

d.) Run the gun along the space you want to fill, clicking the trigger in and out to release the caulking. When you are ready to stop, turn the plunger down, and pull it back to stop the flow. There is a knack to operating a caulking gun with a smooth touch, knowing how much pressure to exert and when to let up. You might, therefore, practice first in an inconspicuous spot.

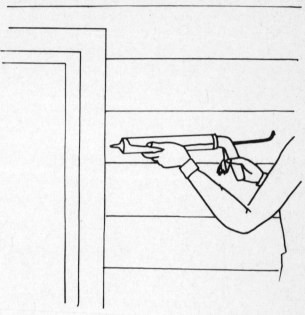

caulking gun

e.) Smooth the caulking into place, where necessary, with your finger. We have found that better than using a standard tool. If you are using latex caulking, wetting your finger with water first is helpful; if the caulking is any of the other types, mineral spirits can be used instead of water.

f.) Clean up any splattering, as well as the caulking gun itself, as soon as you have finished. Again use water as a solvent for the latex kind and mineral spirits for the other varieties.

g.) If any caulking remains in the cartridge, close up the tip of the nozzle tightly. This can be accomplished by stuffing it with something like a large screw.

Regular caulking is installed permanently; thus you won't want to seal your inside windows with it. It will not only keep the winter breezes out, but the summer ones too. Caulking in cord form, which looks and feels like clay, is the ideal product to use as a seasonal measure. It can be applied and removed (even reused) easily. As the box on one brand says, "No tacks or tools—just press into place." It is relatively inconspicuous but can be painted over. Just be aware that, like anything else, once you paint it, it will not peel off as easily as you might like.

Steps: Fiberglass Blanket Insulation

Fiberglass blanket insulation is known for its easy installation primarily because it comes in two widths—15" and 23"—perfectly designed to fit between the studs, rafters, and joists of houses that are built to meet the standard spacing of every 16" or 24". The insulation can be stapled onto the inside surface of each stud because it has a 1" paper flap, called a flange, on each edge.

To install the blankets:

a.) Put on work clothes that include a long sleeved shirt, long pants, and work gloves (a must).

b.) Measure the length of the space where the first strip will go. Cut a piece of insulation with your heavy shears, adding a few inches to the top and bottom. You can also put the strip down, put a plank of wood over it and, using it as a straight edge, cut it with a utility knife.

c.) Where there are no obstructions (pipes, wires, electrical boxes) set the insulation into place between the studs, rafters or joists, foil side facing into the room. When you are working on a wall, the fiberglass should hit the back surface, but if you are insulating a ceiling, leave about 1" of air space.

If you do come to pipes or wires, you must fit the insulation behind them, closer to the outside to protect them from the cold. If you have an outlet or electrical box, you may have to cut the insulation to go around it.

d.) Starting from the top, with that few inches excess, staple the flanges to the inside facing of the wood stud at intervals of about 5". When the sides are in place, stuff the extra material at the top and bottom into the hollow space, and then staple it in place. To do this neatly, you may have to pull the foil down, push the fiberglass in, and staple the paper to the wood. Your aim is to let as little air through the insulation at these seams as possible.

If you tear the foil, which is all too possible, you must repair it, or the insulation will lose some of its effectiveness. If you haul out the ever faithful contact cement, you can take a scrap of foil

stapling the flanges

and glue it onto the damaged spot.

e.) Follow the same process for each successive strip until the entire floor, ceiling, or wall is insulated.

If your studs, joists, or rafters are not regularly spaced at 16" or 24", then you will have to improvise which, in some cases, means running the blankets horizontally between these wood structures. If you feel that you have had to do too much patching, thereby lessening the effectiveness of the insulation, you can cover the entire surface with sheets of clear plastic.

Although at this writing, tax rebates for home insulation are still in the talking stage, the added warmth and the money ultimately saved on heating in the winter and even cooling in the summer are enough incentive. And don't let your do-it-yourself pride be hurt if calling in a professional to blow in loose insulation or install combination storms and screens becomes necessary to make yours a well-insulated home.

Part III

When Not to Do-It-Yourself

Getting Discouraged. At every turn during the course of home buying and renovating, there is some reason for getting depressed or angry or both, and there is little comfort in knowing that it happens to everyone. First, it's seeing house after house that doesn't even vaguely resemble the one you want, and later it's discovering that you need three coats of paint on the dining room walls rather than the usual two, the smooth spackling that you left to dry yesterday has cracked and looks sunken, and the wallpapering job that was supposed to be an evening's entertainment has lasted sixteen hours.

Aside from these personal frustrations, which you may or may not have control over, there are the regular conflicts you face whenever you have to deal with outsiders. It may be the roofers you hired who don't show up on the scheduled day, or the plumber who leaves a pipe uncapped so your house gets flooded when you run water in the sink.

But our pet peeve is what we call the "head-shaking syndrome." Whenever, and we mean that literally, we go to purchase supplies for a renovating job, the salesperson always greets our request by wagging his head back and forth in the negative, indicating that there is no such thing. And nine times out of ten we find out, if we persist, that there is, indeed, such a thing right in stock. Either it may go under another name, or needs further description, or is buried under a pile of boxes, but it's usually there. In plumbing supply houses, lighting fixture stores, lumberyards, paint stores—wherever you go—you are likely to meet up with that wagging head, even from otherwise friendly shopkeepers.

If you are determined to get a job done, you won't be put off by these stumbling blocks, but, certainly, it is discouraging.

Chapter 12

Roofing, Heating, Plumbing, Electrical, Exterior Painting, and Cesspool Work

First Considerations

Is it unorthodox for a book whose theme is do-it-yourself to conclude with an about-face? Actually, if you have been following along with us, chapter by chapter, there have already been several times when we've mentioned individual jobs that we would hire others to do: moving in, knocking down walls, installing combination storms and screens, laying linoleum, and blowing in loose insulation.

Deciding to let someone else do a job for you is not always the coward's or lazy man's way out. Like us, most people who decide to do their own home renovation will not be doing it on a full-time basis. We hold jobs which leave only weekends and vacations for these activities. And unless you have bought a nearly perfect house, you soon conclude that YOU *can't do everything*.

Just as in house hunting, when deciding what to do and what not to do yourself, you should establish priorities, possibly along these lines:

Your Interests: If there is wallpapering and sheetrocking to do, but time for only one; choose the one you like best, and pay someone to do the other.

Your Skills: If you have discovered some ability to work with wood, but have no idea how to fix a leaky pipe; refinish the table yourself, and call a plumber for the leak.

Dangers Involved: If your roof is high and steep, let someone else do the roofing while you paint the walls.

Time Available: If painting the outside of your house will take the entire summer—weekends and vacation time—hire a painter, and accomplish a half dozen smaller tasks yourself.

What you eventually choose to work on or leave to others will, in any case, involve personal and often arbitrary decisions. It was certainly that way for us. We undertook ceramic tiling and floor refinishing which almost everyone we know would go nowhere near, but we did not paint the outside of our house or put up our own roof, two things which you often see people trying on their own.

What follows are brief descriptions of the six major jobs that we decided not to do ourselves. They are *not* included to convince you to go that route too; you will set your own priorities. But since someday, somewhere, you are bound to seek outside help, it is important to know:

—how to get an estimate
—when to check references
—what should go into a written work agreement
—how to deal with contractors
—what to do in emergency situations

As you may already suspect, sitting back and letting someone else do the work is not always the joy you dreamed it would be. You may have sweated and cursed over something you did yourself, but the jobs you turn over to "professionals" can also be fraught with hassles. Perhaps you can learn from our mistakes.

MAJOR PLUMBING WORK

Since some homeowners are graduating from replacing worn washers and ballcock assemblies to more advanced plumbing jobs, one wonders whether this development is what accounts for the great plumbing rip-off customers are getting when they choose not to do the work themselves.

We had done the ceramic tiling, the wallpapering, and the painting in one bathroom ourselves, but the plumbing involved too many rather unusual twists. In our remodeling in reverse, we had decided to rip out a standard tub and contemporary vanity/sink and replace them with an old claw-foot tub and porcelain pedestal-base sink. Both of these were finds that cost us almost nothing, but both of them were shells; they were not outfitted with either the pipes necessary for installation or the fittings to make them operable. We expected to pay handsomely for such work, but the total bill—$525.00 excluding the hardware—left us dumbstruck.

Our mistake was not only failure to get *estimates* from several plumbers; we didn't even have the one we called tell us how much the job was going to cost! No doubt you are thinking that we got exactly what we deserved, and you are right. Our only excuse, admittedly flimsy, was that the plumber (a man whose name we had gotten from a local paper when we once had a minor emergency) used a very subtle form of psychology on us. From the start, head wagging from side to side, he assured us that he was the only one we'd ever find willing to take on the challenge of our job. And we believed him! But don't be as gullible as we were, whether it be with a plumber or any other workman. Regardless of what you are told, unless you are facing an emergency, get several people to come by and give you *written* estimates for the work.

You may end up selecting the person who gave you the lowest estimate, but that will not always be the case. Sometimes a higher price might include additional work or finer materials, and, occasionally, you will just intuitively feel that one person will do a better job, making the extra cost worthwhile.

EXTERIOR PAINTING

This may be the most controversial of the jobs we decided against doing ourselves. We knew that the skills involved could be mastered rather easily, but time, alone, was reason enough for us to reject the idea. We wanted to change the color of the shingles from dark to light which meant at least

two coats, and the endless wood trim needed preparing, as well as repainting. With a three-story house, involving much work on high ladders, we decided that we could accomplish a lot of very necessary interior work if we were to hire a painter for the outside.

Finding painters we could afford, however, was a neat trick. This time we did get several estimates, but after making our choice we should have asked the painters for *references* that we could check. We took the lowest estimate because our money was limited, but the results were somewhat disappointing. The trim was hardly touched before it was repainted, the two coats of paint did not cover every spot, and the paint used faded rather quickly. We did have them redo the most glaring flaws, but much of what we were unhappy with did not show up until after we had paid for the job. For the poor quality workmanship we got from these professionals, we could have easily hired some college students and gotten the same mediocre job done for even less money. Perhaps if we had checked their references, we would have been encouraged to look elsewhere.

INSTALLING A NEW HEATING SYSTEM

Actually, our first dealings with a contractor came shortly after we moved in and discovered that our heating system, although in working condition, was an old, dirty one which threw off lots of soot into the house. Then, as now, we would not have thought to do such work ourselves.

The job we agreed to involved: removing and hauling away our old furnace and installing a new one along with the replacement of some of the ducts. These items as well as some other technical work were formally listed and presented to us in a fancy folder by the contractor. Were we lucky that this company was so precise! The work was one day from completion with only the electrical hookup remaining when the electrician they called in informed us that we did not have sufficient wiring to support the new system. The situation soon snowballed into a major crisis involving the Long Island Lighting Company, the contractor, the electrician, our neighbors and us— homeowner of four months duration. After many sleepless nights, what seemed like a possible court case was resolved on a technicality, and the *con-*

tractor had to bear the cost of putting in a second electrical line, not simply a new circuit. Why? Because in black and white our agreement included the installation of "all required wiring."

Although dramatic events do not always arise every time a contractor steps in, even minor tragedies can be avoided, or at least covered, if everything the company says it will do is put into a *written contract.*

ROOFING

Hiring a locally well-known roofing company did not insure us a very good job, but it surely taught us a lot about dealing with contractors. By this time we knew to get several estimates, check references, and put everything in writing, but we soon found there was more to learn than that. Unfortunately, what you discover is that these salesmen—only in a one-man operation does the person in the suit and tie who comes to your house actually do the physical labor—are excellent double-talkers who usually win whenever you try to confront them with a complaint.

In looking over our contract, several years later, we see the particulars of the agreement spelled out in all the detail anyone would want. When it is written, "Reshingle entire residence using . . . asphalt roofing shingles applied over existing roof shingles," one would hardly think of adding, ". . . so that the surface looks nice and smooth." This is a contract, not a descriptive writing assignment, and, besides, what company would tell you that the new roof might look bumpy?

A few days into the work, we were finally able to make a daylight inspection of their progress, and we were appalled by the wavy surface. We called the roofing company immediately and requested a meeting before we let another shingle be nailed in. We sounded very forceful throughout (they weren't going to put anything over on *us*), but when all was said, we were the losers. In the usual slick manner, the owner of the company explained why our roof, although perfectly secure, could not look smooth. Unless we had wanted to rip off the old roofs and start from scratch, an operation that would cost thousands, we had to be satisfied with what we were getting. Of course we asked him why he didn't tell us what to expect, but it was all in vain. We had very little choice at

that moment, and we have "learned to live with" the results—fortunately, the front looks much better than the back.

What still angers us is that the company never suggested any alternative which might have covered the old roofs more smoothly. Recently we saw someone installing wood shingles instead of asphalt, and we realized what an attractive possibility that could have been. We had chosen an established roofer over a part-time handyman because of the warranties that went along with the work. We guess that, alone, plus the lesson we learned about dealing with contractors—which is that you can't deal with them—was worth at least part of the price we paid.

CESSPOOLS AND SEPTIC TANKS

In a technologically advanced society like ours, cesspools and septic tanks (which serve similar purposes but are constructed differently) have always struck us as rather primitive and, certainly, things one didn't want to spend much time thinking about. No doubt this is the reason why we only deal with them when an *emergency* arises. And an emergency is, naturally, the worse time to get work done on the house. As the pipes are backing up, it is difficult to calmly interview several companies and check their references. You consider yourself lucky just to find someone willing to come that day.

Since it is impossible to prevent the unexpected at all times, whether it be your cesspool or anything else you know you can't handle yourself, try to soften the blow in these ways:

1.) Make a list of the possible services you might someday need to call on (plumber, electrician, cesspool service company, oil burner repair company, chimney sweeper, etc.), and, at your leisure, get a recommendation from a local person for each one.

2.) Look for danger signs, and don't wait until they reach crisis proportions before you get help.

When our cesspool started to back up, even though it was only clear water, we wanted to tend to it immediately. But we had no idea whom to call, and none of our neighbors were home to ask either. All we could do was pick a name at random, from the phone book, and we were lucky to hit upon a reputable firm. Reputable, of course, does not mean that competent work is done at all times; it means only that the company will stand behind its performance and return without charge if something is not fixed properly.

It is difficult for anyone to know exactly what is going on inside a cesspool, so, usually, the first move is to have it Roto-rooted and treated chemically. Just don't let the cesspool people use the chemicals too often; you don't want the tank to be eaten away. The back-up problem we had was given the chemical approach without success. When he returned to honor his written warranty, a lazy serviceman repeated the process rather than find out what was really wrong; fortunately he caused no permanent damage. On the third call, a conscientious worker did some exploring and uncovered the problem: tree roots that had grown into the pipes. Removing them was a major operation that even involved tearing up part of our lawn. The only bright spot was that we were not charged for this expensive job because we had already paid once, a much smaller sum, to have our system repaired.

MAJOR ELECTRICAL WORK

We may have been unwilling to do exterior painting because the technical matters involved too much study, but we have stayed away from major electrical work out of simple but acute fear. We are terrified of forgetting to turn off the power and getting surprise shocks, but we also know how dangerous faulty wiring can be. When we moved into our house we saw some obvious handiwork of do-it-yourself electricians and realized why, according to law in most places, all major electrical work must be done by someone who is licensed in the field. The same, incidentally, is true of plumbing.

Books can teach you how to do all sorts of minor and advanced electrical jobs: replacing a faulty plug, hanging a light fixture, installing new circuits or outlets and rewiring the house, but the local building codes are usually strict about the major work, and we do not recommend violating them. We can, however, understand why someone not quite as intimidated by electricity as we are might want to get involved with it. If plumbers and roofers and painters are costly, electricians must have taught them everything they know. We are used to steep fees, but after *one* day's work cost us over $400, we will wait for an emergency before we call another electrician for quite a while. But since, someday, we know that we will want several outdoor outlets installed, the frost-free refrigerator put on its own circuit, and the switch moved in the bathroom, we know that we will call the electrician again because, in this case, we are still reluctant to do-it-ourselves.

Afterthought:

The Finished Product

Throughout the book we have spoken about the agony involved in each experience, but, luckily, most of us are able to forget pain rather quickly and remember the good things instead. With home renovation, in particular, you have the finished product to enjoy and take pride in long after the aggravation has worn off.

There must develop, between homeowners who do their own restoration and the object of all that attention, the house itself, a very special bond. We can't imagine our own situation to be unique; yet no one else in our acquaintance seems to have a house that is talked about or asked about as much as ours. To be honest, we began it all by telling everyone about our adventures, whereas other people may have kept these things to themselves. Perhaps it was being the first to buy an old house that made the difference, or maybe it was just our excitement that rubbed off on everyone else. But even five years later, all sorts of people, from the school custodian to the instructor at our health spa, regularly ask us, "How's the house coming?"

We don't think anyone ever has a truly "finished product" for, as soon as you think it's all over, you get another bright idea, or else, it's time to redo something that has faded. That, too, is part of the pleasure when a real kinship has developed between you and your house. We used to think it corny, but there really must be something to the old adage, "Home is where the heart is."

GLOSSARY

abrasive A substance used for grinding, polishing, or smoothing, such as steel wool or sandpaper.

batt A rectangular block of fiberglass insulation, faced with aluminum foil or kraft paper.

baseboard molding installed along the bottom of a wall to add a finished appearance.

beam any large, load-bearing piece of lumber, such as a joist or rafter.

bearing wall A wall which helps to carry the weight of the house.

beveled Something cut at a slant or angle, such as a wood chisel or the borders of certain antique mirrors.

binder A token figure, usually between fifty and a few hundred dollars, which a prospective buyer gives the seller, either directly or through a real estate agent. Its purpose is to obligate the seller to hold the house for you for a specified period, at the negotiated price.

binding What happens when your blade gets caught in a saw cut (kerf).

blanket A long, continuous roll of fiberglass insulation, faced with aluminum or kraft paper.

butt To join side to side without overlapping, as with sheets of paneling or strips of wallpaper.

buyers' market A period in the real estate market when there are more people trying to sell their houses than there are people seeking to buy them. The buyer is consequently at an advantage.

casement A hinged window which opens in and out rather than up and down.

chuck The portion of a drill that grabs hold of the bit. You use a chuck key to open and close it.

closing The final step in the purchase of a house when ownership is officially passed from the seller to the buyer.

contract A written document, signed in the presence of the sellers, buyers, and the respective attorneys, which specifies all terms of the sale: full description of the property, selling price, liabilities of both parties, plus additional agreements or addenda.

contractor A company or individual in the building trade who contracts with a homeowner to complete a repair or remodeling job.

countersink To sink the head of a screw or nail so it lies level with or below the working surface.

deposit A portion of the down payment payable to the seller when the contracts are drawn up.

down payment The amount of money paid to the sellers of the house which the buyers put down in cash at the time of purchase.

double hung Standard windows, in most homes, that open up and down and are controlled by a system of weights and pulleys.

enamel A paint that covers a surface with a smooth and glossy coat.

escrow Money deposited with some third party which cannot be withdrawn until certain contractual obligations are met.

exclusive The real estate broker alleges that the house offered for sale is being offered for sale through his office only.

FHA mortgage A Federal Housing Administration loan, a kind of mortgage best suited to families with a limited amount of money available for a down payment.

flange The flap along both edges of fiberglass insulation which is stapled into the studs or rafters.

flush Butted; placed directly up against an adjacent surface.

furring Narrow strips of wood nailed in a continuous framework over the studs in a wall to provide a base for sheetrock, paneling, etc.

girder   A principal beam that supports a floor or partition.

glazier's points   Small metal triangles used to hold glass in place in a window as you apply glazing compound.

grain   Direction of the fibers that make up the substance of a piece of wood. Sanding of floors and furniture should be done *with* the grain, whenever possible.

grout   A thin cement used to fill the spaces between already installed ceramic tile.

hollow wall   An interior wall built from studs and faced with either plaster, sheetrock, paneling, etc.

jamb   The pieces of wood surrounding the tops and sides of a door or window.

joist   Parallel boards nailed at right angles to the framing lumber of a house. This supports the floors and ceilings.

laquer   A high-gloss, quick-drying clear finish for furniture. Lacquer is usually sprayed professionally.

latex   A water-base paint of synthetic rubber.

lath   Narrow strips of wood nailed to the joists or studs to provide a base for plastering or tiling.

lien   An unmet obligation owed to a creditor by the owners of a particular piece of property. A lien is said to be attached to the property until the obligation is cleared.

masonry   Stonelike substances, including brick, concrete, cement, ceramic tile, etc.

miter   To cut on a diagonal at the ends of two pieces of wood that are to be joined at a corner.

molding   Decorative wood trim used most often where the walls meet the floors and ceilings.

mortgage   Conventional: A bank loan given to a prospective home buyer at the currently specified rate of interest towards the purchase price of a house.   FHA: A mortgage held by the Federal Housing Administration.   Takeover: The new owner continues to make payments towards the former owner's existing mortgage with the remainder of the selling price paid outright in cash.

mullions   Narrow strips of wood that separate the panes of glass in a double hung window.

multiple listing   A house for sale is offered through one agency, but a copy of the offer and a picture of the house are sent to several other agencies that are part of a multiple listing service.

negotiating price   The so-called "asking price" which the sellers allege they want for the purchase of their house. This figure is usually subject to bargaining.

non-bearing wall (partition)   Generally speaking, a hollow wall that divides the rooms inside a house. Non-bearing walls do not help to support the basic structure.

on center   To calculate the distance between joists, studs, etc., by measuring from the center of one to the center of the other.

perimeter   The measurement around the outer boundaries of an object.

penny   Originally, the number of pennies one paid for a hundred nails. Today, a description of nail size. 6d (sixpenny) = 2", 8d - 2½", 10d = 3", etc.

pilot hole (starter hole)   A small hole bored into a piece of wood, either with an awl or a drill bit, to ease the insertion of a screw.

plumb   Perfectly vertical.

polyurethane A durable, synthetic varnish for use on floors, countertops, and furniture.

primer A base coat of paint applied to a raw wood or metal surface to prepare it for the finishing coats.

principals only A real estate term meaning that the owners of a house are offering it for sale directly to prospective buyers, without the services of a broker.

quarter round Molding used in corners and along baseboard trim to lend a finished appearance.

R value A measure of the heat resistance of fiberglass insulation. Generally the higher the R value, the better and more efficient job the insulation does.

sash The frame of a window which holds the glass.

sealer A finishing liquid diluted in its own solvent that is applied to newly sanded wood in order to close the pores.

sellers' market A period in the real estate market when there are more people looking to buy houses than there are people who want to sell them. The seller is consequently at an advantage.

shellac Lac resin dissolved in alcohol and used as a sealer or finish for wood.

shim A thin piece of cardboard or wood inserted behind a furring strip or elsewhere in order to obtain a level surface or equalize an imbalance.

solid wall Usually an exterior wall, constructed from some type of masonry: stone, concrete, cinder blocks, or brick.

solvent Something which thins or dissolves a liquid.

stain A pigment brushed on or rubbed into a wood surface to deepen the color.

stop A molding around the edges of doors or windows to hold them in proper position when closed.

stud Parallel timbers, usually spaced 16" on center, which are the framing members of a wall.

subfloor Wood nailed to the floor joists. This provides a base for the installation of the finished hardwood flooring.

tack rag A rag dipped in mineral spirits and a small amount of a finishing material to remove lint or dust from a newly finished piece of furniture.

title A certificate of exclusive ownership of a piece of property.

title search A procedure carried out by a title company which defines the boundaries of the property being sold.

tongue and groove Lumber, generally used in floors or wall panels, designed so that a protruding notch (the tongue) fits into its neighbor's groove.

vapor barrier Facing material (usually aluminum foil) on blankets of fiberglass insulation to keep water vapor from penetrating the walls.

varnish Resins, dissolved in alcohol or oil, used as a lustrous wood finish.

weather stripping Strips of material made of metal, felt, vinyl, or foam which can be used around doors, windows, baseboard moldings, etc. to provide added insulation.

Index